Clockwise from bottom: B&W still from THE LAST WAR; the Diet Building pre and post apocalypse; GORATH Bromide card; and screengrabs from THE LAST WAR, GORATH (with Yumi Shirakawa and Kumi Mizuno) and GENO-CIDE THE LAST WAR © 1961 TOHO CO., LTD. GORATH © 1962 TOHO CO., LTD. GENOCIDE © 1968 SHOCHIKU.

映画の裏側
大特撮

FEATURES

EDITORIAL...6

SAKYO KOMATSU Mini-bio on Japan's most celebrated sci-fi author...8

BEFORE JAPAN SANK Take a look at all the pre-1973 Japanese 'Panic Movies' like Toei's THE FINAL WAR (1960); Toho's THE LAST WAR (1961) and GORATH (1962); plus Shochiku's GENOCIDE (1968). Includes unmade projects like JAPANESE APACHE and INTER ICE AGE 4...10

JAPAN SINKS Learn about the road to 1973's landmark SUBMERSION OF JAPAN plus a review of the film...28

SCRIPTING JAPAN SINKS Explore the differences between the book and the movie...32

JAPAN SINKS IN AMERICA A comprehensive comparison between the Japanese cut and TIDAL WAVE...40

JAPAN SINKS ON TV Summary and episode guide for the 1974-1975 television version...56

AFTER JAPAN SINKS The rundown on PROPHECIES OF NOSTRADAMUS (1974); THE BULLET RAIN (1975); CONFLAGRATION (1975); VIRUS (1980) and other 'Panic Movies' up to TOKYO BLACKOUT (1987)...66

THE LOST FILMS FANZINE PRESENTS MOVIE MILESTONES, VOL. 2, #3 WINTER 2021

EDITOR AND PUBLISHER: JOHN LEMAY/BICEP BOOKS SPECIAL CONSULTANT: KYLE BYRD SPECIAL THANKS THIS ISSUE TO JULES CARROZZA, KEVIN DERENDORF AND TED JOHNSON

MOVIE MILESTONES IS A SPECIAL MAGAZINE PUBLISHED IN CONJUNCTION WITH THE LOST FILMS FANZINE. THE COPYRIGHTS AND TRADEMARKS OF THE IMAGES FEATURED HEREIN ARE HELD BY THEIR RESPECTIVE OWNERS. MOVIE MILESTONES ACKNOWLEDGES THE RIGHTS OF THE CREATORS AND THE COPYRIGHT HOLDERS OF THE IMAGES THEREIN AND DOES NOT SEEK TO INFRINGE UPON THOSE RIGHTS. IMAGES AND MATERIALS USED HEREIN ARE PUBLICITY IMAGES THAT WERE MADE AVAILABLE FOR MAGAZINE USE AT THE TIME OF THE RESPECTIVE FILMS RELEASES AND ARE USED IN THE INTEREST OF EDUCATION AND PUBLICITY. ARTICLES AND TEXT WITHIN THE MAGAZINE ARE © THEIR RESPECTIVE AUTHORS AND MAY NOT BE REPRINTED WITHOUT PERMISSION. MOVIE MILESTONES IS NOT ASSOCIATED WITH TOHO CO., LTD. TOEI STUDIO CO., LTD. OR KADOKAWA/DAIEI STUDIO CO., LTD. COVER IMAGES: TIDAL WAVE © 1975 TOHO CO., LTD./NEW WORLD PICTURES (PREMIUM COLOR VERSION); PROPHECIES OF NOSTRADAMUS © 1974 TOHO CO. LTD. (BASIC COLOR VERSION); THE BULLET TRAIN © 1975 TOEI STUDIO CO., LTD. (BLACK AND WHITE VERSION) CONTACT THE EDITOR @ jplemay@plateautel.net

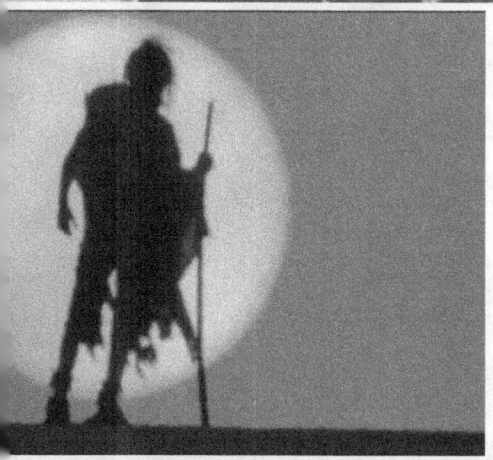

Clockwise from bottom: VIRUS's most famous shot; the stars of PROPHECIES OF NOSTRADAMUS; Japanese magazine spread for CONFLAGRATION; Tetsuro Tamba in SUBMERSION OF JAPAN; storyboard for SUBMERSION; miniature for SUBMERSION; and a European lobby card for PROPHECIES OF NOSTRADAMUS. VIRUS © 1980 KADOKAWA PULISHING/TOHO CO., LTD. PROPHECIES OF NOSTRADAMUS © 1974 TOHO CO., LTD. CONFLAGRATION © 1975 TOHO CO., LTD.

EDITORIAL

I know, I know. I said issue #3 would be devoted to *Gorgo, Konga*, and *Reptilicus* (the monsters of 1961). Well, good news, it's still coming, and that will be issue #4. And, for even more good news: there's going to be four issues of *The Lost Films Fanzine Presents Movie Milestones* this year. Why? Well, last year I really didn't know what I was doing. This was all an experiment. For a while I contemplated upping *The Lost Films Fanzine* to six issues per year in 2021, and keeping *Movie Milestones* at only two. Ultimately, I kept getting too many good ideas for *Movie Milestones* to limit it to only two issues per year, so I compromised. *Lost Films Fanzine* would stay quarterly (four issues a year) but *Movie Milestones* would bump up to the same number. So there you go.

You might next ask why there's even a need for two separate magazines. Well, number one it's a free country and I need something to do when I get bored. But, more importantly, I really don't want to do too many theme issues of the main 'zine. I like to keep that one wild and eclectic, where you never know what you might find. This magazine, on the other hand, is all about themes and anniversaries. The layout, I hope you might notice, is also a little nicer than the main 'zine too I guess you could call it a collector fanzine. Something to cherish for the ages rather than chuck into the dumpster when you're done reading it.

You might also be wondering why did this issue become #3 instead of Gorgo and co as promised? That's because I really, really wanted to write about an oft neglected genre called the Japanese 'Panic Movie,' the equivalent of the American disaster movie made popular in the 1970s. And while the uneducated might be thinking that 'Panic Movies' were inspired by disaster movies, they were not. They actually precede them by one year. Toho's landmark *Submersion of Japan* came out in 1973, one year before *Earthquake* in 1974. *Submersion* sparked a mini-wave of 'Panic Movies' in Japan that included one of the most famous 'lost films' of all time: *Prophecies of Nostradamus* (1974). The film was a huge hit in Japan, and even received the endorsement of the Japanese Education Council for its stance on pollution problems. However, despite that endorsement and its runaway success at the box office, the film has never received a proper home video release. Not on VHS, not DVD, not Blu-Ray. Nada. The reason why was because the film's ending scene showed two mutant humans, scarred and deformed by radiation, which drew the ire of a 'No Nukes' group which labeled it offensive and boycotted the film. As such, the film stays locked in the Toho vault to this day.

Actually, most of the films covered in this issue lack a proper home video release in the U.S. *Submersion of Japan's* U.S. version, called *Tidal Wave*, never saw a VHS release. Nor has the Japanese cut ever been released to DVD/Blu-Ray in the west which is a true shame for film lovers, as it's fantastic.

More so than any of the other Panic Movies in this issue we're going to focus on *Submersion of Japan*, as it was the kick-starter of the genre (though we will also cover it's ancestors, like 1961's *The Last War*). You may have noticed that this is not an anniversary year for the film. (Yes, I know, I could've waited two years for 2023 to roll around and make it a 50th anniversary issue, but you have to remember, we're coming off our own mini-apocalypse of 2020, and I don't want to wait that long lest a real Panic Movie plays out in the next few years). But, the lack of the film's anniversary won't stop me. I did some digging and found out that on January 28th of this year that the creator of *Submersion of Japan*, the legendary Sakyo Komatsu, would have turned 90. Therefore, this is a Sakyo Komatsu tribute issue as much as it is about Japanese Panic Movies.

One more word before we depart: a good chunk of this issue is cannibalized from a little book I wrote called *Terror of the Lost Tokusatsu Films*. There, I admitted it. But, that book has not sold well, so chances are you haven't read it anyways. So, hopefully, this will all be new to you. But if you have read that book don't fret, there's still plenty of new content in this issue, from a detailed comparison between *Submersion of Japan* and *Tidal Wave*, an episode guide for the *Submersion* TV show, a brand new write up on *The Monkey Army, Virus, Bullet Train* and lots more!

-John LeMay, November 2020

On January 28, 1931, in Osaka was born landmark sci-fi author Minoru "Sakyo" Komatsu. Of all the Japanese science fiction writers, Sakyo Komatsu is the best known outside of his native country. This is in large part because several of his epics were adapted into Japanese films that were also released in America, like *Submersion of Japan* (1973, in the U.S. as *Tidal Wave* in 1975) and *Day of Resurrection* (1980, as *Virus* in the U.S.).

Komatsu studied Italian literature at Kyoto University and was a fan of writers like Kobo Abe, author of *Inter Ice Age 4*, a novel with a few similarities to *Submersion of Japan*. Before striking it big as an author, Komatsu worked as a reporter and even wrote material for some stand-up comics. In 1961 he entered his short story, "Pacem in Terris," in a contest in *SF Magazine*. Though he didn't win, he received an honorable mention and ¥5,000 from Toho Studios (the sponsor).

In 1962, his story "Memoirs of an Eccentric Time Traveler" was published in *SF Magazine*. Sometime after this, he also helped in the planning stages of Tsuburaya Productions burgeoning sci-fi series, later to be known as *Ultra Q*. In 1964 his first novel, *Japanese Apache*, sold a remarkable 50,000 copies and was almost adapted into a film by Toho. That same year, Komatsu also published *Day of Resurrection* which one day would be made as a movie, albeit 16 years later.

Komatsu's next near-miss with motion pictures came when Toho planned on adapting his manga *ESPY* in 1967. That film too would eventually be made some years later after the success of the movie adaptation of *Submersion of Japan* (1973). The novel was a huge hit in Japan and was later even released in the U.S. in 1975 at the same time that *Tidal Wave* was in theaters.

Komatsu was impressed by the fact that his novel had been translated into English, but not by the translation itself, which not only omitted scenes but also misinterpreted them. Komatsu told *Science Fiction Studies* that, "One [mistake] I noticed right away is in the part where the old man Watari is staying with Dr. Tadokoro at the villa on Lake Ashinoko. The translator mistook Ashinoko for the name of a woman. [Laughs] The scene is supposed to take place on a lake in the mountains of Hakone, but suddenly it was as if we had been transported to a hostess bar in Ginza!"[www.depauw.edu/sfs/backissues/88/komatsuinterview.htm]

After the success of *Submersion of Japan*, in 1974, Komatsu's *ESPY* was dusted off by Toho and finally put to film. That same year, Komatsu also worked as a writer for Tsuburaya Productions TV series *The Monkey Army* (released as a compilation movie in the U.S. called

THE LOST FILMS FANZINE PRESENTS MOVIE MILESTONES #3

On July 21st of that year, *Sakyo Komatsu Magazine* quoted its namesake's thoughts on the disaster. Komatsu said, "I had thought I wouldn't mind dying any day ... but now I'm feeling like living a little bit longer and seeing how Japan will go on hereafter." Komatsu died five days later on July 26, 2011, in Osaka at the age of 80. The cause was complications from pneumonia.

Time of the Apes in 1987). Around this time Komatsu also worked with Toho in trying to come up with a sequel to *Submersion of Japan*, though the film never happened (the sequel, *Japan Sinks, Part II*, in novel form, was finally published in 2006).

Komatsu's next film adaptation was *Day of Resurrection* in 1980, starring the likes of George Kennedy, Glenn Ford, and other well-known Hollywood stars. Before that, in lieu of the success of *Star Wars*, Tomoyuki Tanaka had asked Komatsu to come up with a space opera for him. The fruits of this labor weren't published until 1982 as *Sayonara Jupiter*, which was filmed by Komatsu himself for Toho in 1984. Like Steven King on *Maximum Overdrive*, Komatsu more or less helped to direct *Sayonara Jupiter* and had almost complete creative control on the project (except for the budget that is). The film was a flop, as was the next Komatsu-inspired film: *Tokyo Blackout* (1987).

Komatsu lived long enough to see *Submersion of Japan* remade by Shinji Higuchi in 2006 as *Japan Sinks*. Komatsu also ironically lived to see the Tohoku earthquake and tsunami of 2011 which he quasi-predicted in *Submersion of Japan*.

SELECTED FILMOGRAPHY/ BIBLIOGRAPHY

Matango (1963) (uncredited ideas)
Japanese Apache (1964) [novel]
Day of Resurrection (1964) [novel]
ESPY (1965) [manga]
Ultra Q (1966) [TV series]
(development work)
Japan Sinks (1973) [novel]
Submersion of Japan (1973)
(based upon the novel)
ESPY (1974)
(based upon the manga)
The Monkey Army (1974) [TV series]
(writer)
Japan Sinks (1974) [TV series]
(based upon the novel)
Tidal Wave (1975)
(based upon the novel)
Day of Resurrection/Virus (1980)
(based upon the novel)
Sayonara Jupiter (1982) [novel]
Sayonara Jupiter (1984)
(writer, producer, director)
Tokyo Blackout (1985) [novel]
Tokyo Blackout (1987)
(based upon the novel)
Japan Sinks (2006)
(based upon the novel)
Japan Sinks, Part II (2006) [novel]
Japan Sinks, Part III
[concept, uncompleted]

BEFORE JAPAN SANK:

It could probably be argued that Japan's first 'Panic Movie' (though the term had yet to be invented) was Daiei's 1956 movie *Warning From Space*. Similar to George Pal's *When Worlds Collide* (1951), the film had the runaway Planet R about to collide with Earth until friendly starfish aliens intervene and save mankind. However, due to its far-out sci-fi elements, most scholars group it in with sci-fi alien invader films. Most fans would probably argue that Toei's 1960 film *The Final War* was the first Japanese disaster/panic movie. Often mistaken for Toho's similar but better-known *The Last War* (1961), the case of *The Final War* and its "twin" is comparable in many ways to dueling projects in Hollywood.

For instance, back in 1998, the U.S. box office was astir wondering just which asteroid movie would win out: Michael Bay's *Armageddon* or Mimi Leder's *Deep Impact*. Despite both films having the same subject matter, neither suffered at the box office as a result. Other instances of similar competing films included when Roger Moore's Bond film *Octopussy* was released the same year as Sean Connery's 007 movie *Never Say Never Again* in 1983. As stated earlier, back in 1960 Japan, Toho and Toei both had end of the world movies in development at the same time. Like the aforementioned blockbusters, both films were released relatively close to one another and both were hits.

The Final War and *The Last War* were not surprisingly both born out of a story published in the *Weekly Shincho*, called "First 41 Hours of World War III" published in the summer of 1960 (*The Final War* was initially entitled *World War III: 41 Hours of Fear* by Toei). As it happened, Toho producer Tomoyuki Tanaka took note of "First 41 Hours of World War III" at the same time that Toei did. Furthermore, Toei Studios beat Tanaka to officially securing the film rights from the author. Unfortunately, Toho didn't know this, and a script was written before they found out about Toei's deal, because the first draft of *The Last War* is remarkably similar to Toei's *The Final War*.

Specifically, Toho's first script for the project was written July 29, 1960, by Shinobu Hashimoto and Toshio Yasumi, and the project was approved for production at the Toho National Branch Chairperson's Board of Directors' meeting on August 8th. Only a few days earlier Toei had also had their shareholders meeting on the 6th where they announced production of their film, *The Final War*. The *Mainichi Newspaper* heard about the dueling projects and soon reported on the brewing competition between the two studios. As a result, Toho shut down their version for a time to rework the script and as a

A TALE OF TWO WARS

result, Toei's version beat Toho's to theaters in October of 1960.

Toho called in several experts to help consult on the second draft of the script, including Nori University professor Keijiro Irie, a prominent authority on international law as well as Toshio Shinzo, a member of the New Interview Study Team and an expert on the military. The second draft was completed on August 11th, only three days after Toho announced the film for production. However, this draft was still incredibly similar to Toei's. By this time, and due to the similarities, Tanaka quit trying to beat Toei's release and had Yasumi and Hashimoto do a rewrite on the script to shake any similarities that could lead to legal action.

On September 2nd, Toshio Yasumi and Shinobu Hashimoto turned in a third draft script, which Toho President Iwao Mori feared was still too close to Toei's version and decided to stop production on September 7, 1960. However, the project wasn't considered dead just yet. Yasumi, this time without Hashimoto, turned in a fourth draft script at an unknown date in 1961 as well as a fifth draft script. The sixth and f i n a l draft was turned in by Takeshi Kimura on June 26, 1961, so that production could finally commence. Though Toei's film had by this time been released more than 6 months ago, Toho had an edge in that their film would not only feature more effects scenes than Toei's, but also be filmed in color.

One last hurdle arose in the form of the original director for *The Last War*, Hironobu Horikawa. The director had been invited to join the project via an urgent telegram from Toho while he was returning to his hometown of Kyoto. However, Horikawa balked at the number of effects sequences and Toho considered the effects scenes to be very important in lieu of the recent success of *Mothra* in in the summer of 1961. As such, Shue Matsubayashi was brought in as the new director. Ultimately *The Final War* didn't hurt Toho's film at all and it was a success.

Toho would follow with another disaster epic in 1962, *Mysterious Star Gorath* about a giant asteroid about to destroy earth. Daiei then did a hurricane movie, *Wind Veloity 75 Meters* in 1963. Directed by Shigeo Tanaka (who would go on to direct *Gamera vs. Barugon* in 1966), it covered an oncoming typhoon. Naturally, the climax was an effects spectacular directed by Yonesaburo Tsukiji wherein Tokyo is partially destroyed by the typhoon. (An entire miniature set of Ginza was built for the typhoon scene and 15 tons of water was dropped onto the miniature set and ended up damaging the soundstage.) Other than that, the last quasi-disaster movie to come out before 1973's *Submersion of Japan* would be Shochiku's *Genocide* (1968).

THE LOST FILMS FANZINE PRESENTS MOVIE MILESTONES #3

THE FINAL WAR

Release Date: October 19, 1960

DIRECTED BY: Shigeaki Hidaka SPECIAL EFFECTS BY: Shigeaki Hidaka & Shozo Konishi SCREENPLAY BY: Hisataka Kai & Shigeaki Hidaka (treatment) MUSIC BY: Ko Ishimatsu CAST: Tatsuo Umemiya (Shigero), Yoshiko Mita (Tomoko), Yayoi Furusato, Noribumi Fujishima, Yukiko Nikaido, Michiko Hoshi

Toeiscope, Black & White, 77 Minutes

SYNOPSIS As Cold War tensions mount, a group of high schoolers led by Shigero flee Japan in a yacht. When the yacht is overtaken by a typhoon, they are rescued by reporter Masaaki, who makes the story front page news. Around the same time, Masaaki begins dating Tomoko, a nurse in Tokyo. Tensions mount when a U.S. air force plane accidentally detonates a nuclear bomb over South Korea, who in turn blames North Korea. This cranks Cold War tensions up to a fever pitch. The U.S. 7th Fleet mobilizes at a base in Japan and soon, a U.S. plane is shot down over the Soviet Union. The Soviet Union warns Japan that all air bases in Japan will be bombed. Masaaki, Shigero, and his family flee to the forest while Tomoko elects to stay behind with a sick child patient in Tokyo. The city is bombed as the evacuees watch from the wilderness. A panicked Masaaki braves Tokyo's radiation to search for Tomoko, whom he finds dead next to her patient. Masaaki himself dies from the radiation exposure soon after.

OVERVIEW: In comparing Toei's *The Final War* to Toho's more widely seen *The Last War*, it's tough to say which of the two is more effective. Though Toho's version is in color and has more effects scenes, Toei's version is actually more grounded. For instance, whereas Toho chose to mask America and Russia in the form of renaming them the Confederation and the Alliance, here the real superpowers are at play.

Though Toho's film is no picnic, Toei's still manages to be darker and grimmer, due both to the ugly portrayals of the evacuating peoples of Tokyo and the black and white photography. During the evacuation, mankind's lesser nature is emphasized and some women are implied to be taken away to be raped. The film's first post-opening credits scene is even a showcase of graphic real-life photos of starving and injured children, making this a stylistic precursor of sorts to *Prophecies of Nostradamus* (1974)— itself a spiritual remake of Toho's *The Last War*.

In *The Last War*, the story is told through the eyes of one family, while in *The Final War* several different families, each in a different economic stratosphere, are portrayed. This works well for the climax, as we see how different groups handle the devastating tension as they wait for Tokyo to be bombed. The low income family, consisting of a musician and his sick wife, go to a Catholic church. Tomoko, the nurse, sings to her sick child patient. Some of the people in the hills go mad with anxiety waiting for the bomb to drop.

The effects scenes are sparser compared to *The Last War*, but it doesn't detract from the film at all. In fact, it almost makes it seem more realistic than the overly colorful effects of *The Last War*. The destruction of the Diet Building is probably the best shot in the film but unfortunately, it's the only major effects shot representing the destruction of Tokyo (aside from a brief glimpse of Tokyo Tower also being destroyed). Brief but well-done shots of miniatures representing New York, San Francisco, and Moscow State University exploding follow. There are some well-done miniatures of a destroyed Tokyo as well, on par with a similar shot from *Godzilla* (1954). And while *The Last War* ended with a statement that the film was merely a "what if" scenario, *The Final War* has no such closing remarks to brighten it up.

The Final War was supposedly released theatrically in the U.S. by Sam Lake Enterprises in 1962 but it's also possible it went straight to television. In any case, no prints of the U.S. version have been found nor was it ever released to VHS. Today, it is difficult to prove whether or not this actually occurred (though there are people adamant they saw it on television). In his *Apocalypse Then*, Mike Bogues writes:

Proof that the movie at least showed in the New York City area is a license to exhibit it in New York State dated December 3, 1962 (this information came from the AFI website). Further proof that the movie at least showed in the New York City area is a brief mention in 1964's *Castle of Frankenstein* #4's "Frankenstein Movie Guide": "Widescreen WW3, destruction of world in atomic war. Japanese made." Later, *Castle of Frankenstein* #9 offered this brief review in its

---

NOTES ON A SHABBY CUFF—Independent distributor Arthur Davis and mighty MGM are about to have at one another with a couple of Japanese movies that deal with the end of the world.

MGM will release Toho Studio's "The Last War" sometime in March, but Davis, who has bought Stateside distribution rights to the Toei film "48 Hours of Fear" (which he has retitled "The Final War") hopes to have his flick on the market in the next month or so.

Davis, in conjunction with Asian Film Inc., has dubbed his movie in English and added a few scenes (he plans to add five or ten minutes more of footage in the States). Dubbing on "The Final War" is pretty good but the picture itself pales beside the more imaginative Toho version of how the world is blown to smithereens.

"Frankenstein TV Movieguide": "Japanese sf mainly of interest because familiar landmarks get the total destruction treatment." [PP.266]

To further confound matters, many who saw the movie on American television swear the film included edited-in footage of U.F.O.s from Toei's more fantastical *Invasion of the Neptune Men* (1961)! It is entirely possible that *The Final War* was released theatrically more or less the same film, just dubbed into English, while Medallian TV Enterprises created a new version for television viewings with said *Neptune Men* footage edited in to better appeal to the kiddie audience.

Oddly, the film has been just as obscure in Japan as it has been in the U.S. For decades, *The Final War* was considered a lost movie. Toei eventually discovered a print and began airing it on Japanese television in 2013, though no DVD or Blu-ray release has been forthcoming. Whether it played in U.S. theaters or not, the U.S. version of *The Final War* is almost certainly gone. As far as anyone knows, the last time it aired on television was back in 1974.

THE LAST WAR

Release Date: October 08, 1961
Alternate Titles: *Great World War* (Japan) *The Last War of the Apocalypse* (France) *Death Rays from Outer Space* (Germany)

DIRECTED BY: Shue Matsubayashi
SPECIAL EFFECTS BY: Eiji Tsuburaya
SCREENPLAY BY: Toshio Yasumi & Takeshi Kimura MUSIC BY: Ikuma Dan
CAST: Frankie Sakai (Mokichi Tamura), Akira Takarada (Takano), Yuriko Hoshi (Saeko Tamura), Nobuko Otowa (Mother Tamura), Yumi Shirakawa (Sanae), Shu Ryuchi (Ehara), Jerry Ito (Watkins), So Yamamura (Prime Minister)

Tohoscope, Eastmancolor, 110 Minutes

SYNOPSIS Mokichi Tamura is a simple but ambitious limo driver who works hard to provide for his family and he has begrudgingly just given his daughter Saeko permission to marry her sweetheart, naval officer Takano. All the while, two world superpowers, the Federation and the Alliance, stockpile nuclear weapons as Cold War tensions rise. When an accident starts World War III, Tokyo is one of the first cities slated to be destroyed. The Tamura family chooses not to evacuate and enjoys one last dinner together before the city is destroyed, while Takano helplessly watches Tokyo destroyed from the sea. The rest of the world, as well, is wiped out in a nuclear holocaust.

OVERVIEW: For fans of the military confrontations in the Godzilla films, in terms of special effects, *The Last War* essentially amounts to a two-hour version of one of those scenes, only instead of battling Godzilla, Tsuburaya's miniature tanks and fighter jets battle each other. However, in terms of human drama, it naturally far eclipses the Godzilla films. In fact, it is a very powerful film and has an even greater anti-nuclear message than *Godzilla* (1954).

The film's heart and soul is comedic actor Frankie Sakai, who works hard to provide for his wife and three children. Contrasting the dreams of this simple man are the escalating tensions of two world superpowers, obvious stand-ins for the U.S. and the Soviets, called the Federation and the Alliance. Though some say Sakai was miscast, seeing a cheerful comedic actor in such a tragic film makes it all the more powerful. The best scene involves Sakai and his family in a deserted Tokyo, evacuated due to threats of nuclear war, having one last family dinner together. Sakai remains in a state of denial, reminding his sick wife to take her medicine even though it is pointless while his eldest daughter pines for her husband Takano, played by Akira Takarada, who is out to sea. Finally, Sakai has a breakdown feeling that all his hard work has been for nothing. And then the film pulls no punches; when the nukes fly, it is for real—there is no epilogue revealing it all to be a "what if" scenario as in *Prophecies of Nostradamus* (1974). Sakai and his loveable family do perish in Tokyo and adding to the tragedy is the fact that Takano actually survives because he is out to sea, knowing full well his wife must be dead. Furthermore, he and his shipmates all decide to return to Tokyo even though they know it means a slow death by radiation poisoning.

The effects in this film are somewhat hit or miss unless one is a diehard miniature enthusiast. There is a bevy of fantastic miniature sets, from nuclear missile bases in the North Pole to nearly every famous landmark imaginable—including the Kremlin, the Statue of Liberty, the Arc De Triumph and more—exploding spectacularly. In this sense, the film is like a much more poignant version of a Roland Emmerich disaster film, albeit set in the 1960s. As stated earlier, this film was released just after a similar film from Toei, *The Final War* in 1960, though *The Last War* has the edge on its competitor due to being filmed in color along with Tsuburaya's effects work.

Amidst all the exploding landmarks, the film's strongest visual may actually be shots of charred bodies, whose ashy remains blow away in the wind—powerful and explicit imagery for 1961 (and strongly invoking memories of Hiroshima and Nagasaki). The film grossed ¥284,000,000 when released to Japanese theaters. In America, the film was released to theaters in 1965 through Brenco. The more well-known television version, cut down to only 79 minutes, made its way to television in 1967.

The Last War is a film that deserves to be remembered better than it is. It may even beat *Godzilla* (1954) as one of the greatest anti-nuke films of all time—in this author's opinion at least. Of course, if you just have to have a giant monster destroying a city, this film may not interest you. But if you're willing to give the story a try it's worth viewing.

SPFX OF THE LAST WAR Eiji Tsuburaya's climax, where the entire world is consumed by nuclear war, is famous for its destruction of famous cities and landmarks, namely miniatures of Moscow, New York, Tokyo, London, and Paris. To film these scenes, the miniatures—made of cake, a technique re-used for the destruction of the White House in INDEPENDENCE DAY—were actually positioned upside down and then blown to bits with compressed air rather than gunpowder. Being upside down, the debris naturally blew downwards, or rather upwards, on screen thanks to camera trickery. In all, Toho spent $830,000 on the miniature sets. This footage was reused many times, first on TV for the series finale of ULTRASEVEN. It was later used in 1974's PROPHECIES OF NOSRADAMUS to portray nuclear annihilation and later even aliens attacked the world via this footage for 1977's THE WAR IN SPACE. Stock footage of Tokyo in lava was used as late as 1995 in several teaser trailers for GODZILLA VS. DESTROYAH.

ALL IMAGES FROM THIS SPREAD FROM THE LAST WAR © 1961 TOHO CO., LTD.

THE LAST WAR'S FIRST DRAFT In Toho's first draft of THE LAST WAR, Saeko was a nurse. The Tamura family would have also fled from Tokyo to escape the bomb rather than staying inside the city. Takano was to try and convince Saeko to leave with him, but she wouldn't abandon her patient just as in Toei's movie. Notably, Tamura's wife was also sickly and bedridden, an element that would stay in the finished film despite it being similar to the subplot in THE FINAL WAR. The first draft also explicitly identified the U.S. and the Soviet Union as in Toei's film, but subsequent drafts would change the names to "the Federation" and "the Alliance" to make the movie easier to market internationally.

THE LOST FILMS FANZINE PRESENTS MOVIE MILESTONES #3

GORATH

Release Date: March 21, 1962
Alternate Titles: *Suspicious Star Gorath* (Japan) *The Shock of the Planets* (France) *U.F.O.s Destroy the Earth* (German) *Threat from the Center of the Universe* (Greece)

DIRECTED BY: Ishiro Honda SPECIAL EFFECTS BY: Eiji Tsuburaya SCREENPLAY BY: Takeshi Kimura MUSIC BY: Kan Ishii CAST: Ryo Ikebe (Dr. Tazawa), Yumi Shirakawa (Tomoko), Akira Kubo (Kanai), Takashi Shimura (Kensuke), Kenji Sahara (Saiki), Kumi Mizuno (Takiko), Jun Tazaki (Captain Sonoda) SUIT PERFORMERS: Haruo Nakajima (Magma)

Tohoscope, Eastmancolor,
88 Minutes

SYNOPSIS In 1979, the research ship JX-1 is sent to investigate a mysterious star, dubbed Gorath, hurtling towards the earth. Unfortunately, Gorath's mass is so deceptively large that the ship is unable to escape the star's gravity. Before it is destroyed, the crew manages to warn earth of the star's trajectory. As nuclear weapons aren't enough to destroy the runaway star, the nations of the world instead band together in the South Pole to build a large rocket propulsion system powerful enough to move the earth out of Gorath's path. The plan is a success and the earth is moved, but Gorath's gravitational pull still causes great damage (such as flooding Tokyo and destroying the moon) as it passes by earth, but at least the planet will survive.

OVERVIEW: Movies about giant asteroids have been a staple of disaster movies for many years and ironically, one of the pioneers of this genre was Toho itself. Even more ironic, perhaps, is that Toho's asteroid was itself monstrous compared to other celluloid asteroids. In fact, it wasn't a true asteroid at all, but a runaway planet!

It would seem that *Gorath* was influenced by *The Last War's* downbeat disaster motif and *Mothra's* fantasy elements. The initial idea was that of Jojiro Okami, who also did the story concepts for *The Mysterians* (1957), *Battle in Outer Space* (1959), and *Space Monster Dogora* (1964). Okami's original story pitch was entitled *Great Earth Modification,* after the effort to modify earth's orbit. Likewise the giant asteroid was originally named Lagos until Toho decided to rename it, discovering it was the name of a city in Nigeria. In the end, rather than moving the earth, the Japanese elite escape earth as the planet is destroyed.

Supposedly, Okami may have pitched the idea as far back as 1959, as *Toho*

U.S. lobby card for GORATH © 1962 TOHO CO., LTD.

Special Effects Movie Complete Works says the developmental process of this film was three years! As was done with *The Mysterians* previously and *Atragon* the next year, Tomoyuki Tanaka insisted a monster be added to the film to spice up the picture. Takeshi Kimura initially added in a run-of-the-mill dinosaur until Ishiro Honda, reluctant to include monsters of any sort in the film, argued a dinosaur was too derivative of Godzilla and so the walrus Magma was created. If Tanaka had hoped the monster would boost the international appeal, it ironically ended up being cut out of the American version from Brenco entirely.

In an attempt to give the picture some scientific accuracy, Ishiro Honda and assistant director Koji Kajita went to the University of Tokyo's Faculty of Science to the Astronomy division. There, they consulted with various experts about how a star of Gorath's size would affect other celestial bodies and if it was remotely possible to alter the earth's orbit. The scientists, specifically Genichiro Hori, felt that moving the earth's orbit was theoretically possible, but did argue that if the moon was sucked into Gorath's orbit the Earth would be sucked in with it. In order to make the earth modification plan seem more realistic, the story was set in the future of 1979 and 1980 (Christmas and New Year's occur in the story), 17 years from 1962.

The cast for the film was top-notch, including established actors such as Ryo Ikebe (*Battle in Outer Space*), Takashi Shimura (*Godzilla*), and Yumi Shirakawa (*Rodan*) along with "new faces" Akira Kubo and Kumi Mizuno who would go on to become big stars at Toho. Kenji Sahara, a favorite of Honda's, was almost cut out of the film and recast when he broke his leg during shooting, but Honda insisted no one else but Sahara play the role. Shooting lasted nearly a whole year at 300 days, 100 of which were allotted just for the special effects.

Overall, the budget was said to be ¥380 million.

The giant pulsating Gorath star was made of acrylic with electric lights that caused it to generate with an angry, orange color. The earth modification scene was one of the more difficult ones to shoot and took Tsuburaya and his crew nearly three weeks according to Teruyoshi Nakano. The huge Antarctica set—where much of the ice was made of Styrofoam—was built inside Toho's Studio No. 8 which covered about 1,652 square meters. The polar rockets were huge and were fueled by a great deal of propane. Due to wind concerns, this sequence had to be filmed on an indoor set which made the studio very hot. Giant walrus Magma was one of the poorer monster costumes created by Tsuburaya's effects department. Magma was inhabited by both Haruo Nakajima and Katsumi Tezuka in different shots.

The props from *Gorath* all had a great deal of longitude. The JX-1 and JX-2 spacecraft models created for this film would appear in several other productions including *Invasion of Astro-Monster* (1965), and even the TV series *Star Wolf* (1978). The space station prop reappeared in *Invasion of Astro-Monster* also. Magma was recycled as the new monster Todora in *Ultra* Q (1966) and almost returned as itself for *Destroy All Monsters* (1968) but didn't make the final roster. Remarkably, the Gorath prop survived for many years and was even used in Koichi Kawakita's *Super Star God* series of the 2000s!

Though it was a big hit, Toho's runaway success with *King Kong vs. Godzilla* later in 1962 would encourage the studio to focus most of their efforts on more giant monster movies, and less so on sci-fi epics like *Gorath*. The film would end up being Toho's last true disaster film for over ten years.

U.S. poster for GORATH (top) and still of Magma (bottom). © 1962 TOHO CO., LTD.

THE LOST FILMS FANZINE PRESENTS MOVIE MILESTONES #3

THE UNMADE FILES: JAPANESE APACHE

Intended Release Date: unknown, presumably 1965
First Draft Date: 1964

SCREENPLAY BY: Nobuo Yamada PROPOSED DIRECTOR: Kihachi Okamoto PROPOSED CAST/CHARACTERS: Kuroda Fukuichi [weapons expert], Jiro Futago [leader of Japanese Apache tribe], Yamada Tansu [political criminal], Urakami [reporter]

SYNOPSIS In an alternative universe version of Post-war Japan, the nation is fully militarized with air, land and sea units. Under this new regime, all Japanese citizens are forced to be hard workers. Being unemployed is a capital offense and violators are banished from society to a barren wasteland in the vicinity of Osaka Prefecture. This fate is considered worse than the death penalty—which has been abolished. Kuroda Fukuichi, who has not found employment quickly enough after having been fired, is banished to this wasteland. Living in this wasteland is a group of survivors, called the Japanese Apache, that have survived and evolved due to eating iron and copper. Kuroda and another exiled man, Yamada, are taken in by the tribe and their leader, Jiro Futago. Kuroda becomes a part of the tribe, and uses his knowledge of weaponry to help the Japanese Apaches lead a revolt against the tyrannical government.

OVERVIEW: If you initially saw this title in the table of contents and assumed it to be some sort of strange, Japanese western, you know that assumption to be incorrect; it is actually a rather unique tale of dystopian Japan. It was also based upon the first novel ever published by the legendary Sakyo Komatsu, who would not long after begin writing *Submersion of Japan*.

Published by Kobunsha Kappa Novels, the book sold an impressive 50,000 copies in 1964 and Toho quickly optioned the book for a film. Komatsu was not hired to adapt his own story though, and that job went instead to Nobuo Yamada who primarily wrote dramas for Nikkatsu in the late 1950s. The proposed director was to be Kihachi Okamoto, who was by this time an accomplished director who would in the future helm *Japan's Longest Day* (1967) and *Blue Christmas* (1978) among many

21

others. Though these two players make sense behind the scenes, the proposed cast most certainly did not. Believe it or not, the Crazy Cats were the actors slated to star in *The Japanese Apache*! The Crazy Cats were a jazz band established in 1955 that eventually went on to star in a series of films for Toho beginning in 1962 and ending in 1971. As most of these films were comedies, it would seem safe to presume that this was to be a comedic adaptation or a legitimate spoof of Komatsu's novel.

That the Crazy Cats would star in this Mad Max-like future wasteland tale seems strange to say the least. But then again, the Japanese Apaches themselves are incredibly strange. Komatsu describes them as a group of scrap iron scavengers that have taken to eating copper and iron! As such, their skin is hard, metallic and copper in color. With their physiology changed due to years of ingesting the metal, they are now stronger and faster than normal humans. Their clothing is described as being similar to Native Americans and they even refer to old cars and motorcycles as livestock! This tribe is democratic, and vote rather than ruling by a dictator, though they do have a chief.

Komatsu's dystopian, labor force- obsessed Japan is also fascinating. It would seem that in this new society that to be unemployed is the greatest sin one can commit. This is also the reason why the protagonist is banished—he hasn't found another job within the allotted time after being fired. This new Japan also possesses a mighty military complete with atomic weapons at its disposal.

Not much is known of the scrapped film adaptation because Komatsu neglects to mention it in his autobiography. From the best that this author can gather, the proposed director Okamoto thought Komatsu's story was too dark. Okamoto even asked another sci-fi novelist, Hirai Kazumasa, to draft a lighter and more fantastical version of the story. Kazumasa was too busy and declined the offer. There was only one draft written by Nobuo Yamada and it is unclear if this was a treatment, a script or a simple story proposal.

The project's cancellation didn't sour Komatsu on Toho though. In an interview with *Science Fiction Studies*, he stated:

When the publishing house Hayakawa Shobo started *SF Magazine* in 1959, they held a contest, the Hayakawa Science Fiction Competition. I sent in the story "Pacem in Terris," and that was the beginning. The sponsor who provided the prize money was the Toho movie studio, which produced *Gojira* [1954]. The condition was that Toho would retain the movie rights to the winning story. That first year of the contest, I received an Honorable Mention and 5000 yen. The second year I shared the prize with Hanmura Ryo, who later won the Naoki Prize. We each got 30,000 yen from Toho, and I felt so obligated [laughs] that in 1973 when we were discussing a film version of *Japan Sinks*, I gave them the movie rights with almost no conditions. I think they paid 1.5 million yen.

And, though *The Japanese Apache* never was adapted into a film, it did become a radio play in 1972.

THE LOST FILMS FANZINE PRESENTS MOVIE MILESTONES #3

THE UNMADE FILES: INTER ICE AGE 4

Intended Release Date: 1966
First Draft Date: September 7, 1965

SCREENPLAY BY: Kobo Abe PRODUCER: Tomoyuki Tanaka PROPOSED DIRECTOR: Hiromichi Horikawa PROPOSED SPFX DIRECTOR: Eiji Tsuburaya PROPOSED CAST/CHARACTERS: Professor Katsumi [inventor], Tanomogi [Katsumi's assistant], Wada [lab worker], Dr. Yamamoto [head of Aquan lab], Tomoyasu [bureaucrat], Mrs. Katsumi [Professor Katsumi's wife]

SYNOPSIS To compete with the world's first super computer, "Moscow-1" in Russia, Japanese scientist Dr. Katsumi creates the "KEIGI-1". The new machine can do everything that the one in Moscow can and more, including replicating people's brainwaves and thought patterns. When Katsumi is forbidden by the government to predict the political future he decides instead to predict the future of a single stranger he sees on the street. Together he and his assistant, Tanomogi, shadow the man and are shocked when the man is later murdered. Katsumi hooks the corpse up to the machine and learns there is more to the murder than meets the eye. Katsumi and Tanomogi learn the man was killed to keep secret the experiments of an organization that specializes in turning land based organisms into aquatic life—including humans. To his horror, Katsumi's own unborn son is taken to become one of the new underwater humans called Aquans. To his shock, this has all been orchestrated by KEIGI-1 itself along with Tanomogi. As KEIGI-1 has Katsumi's thought patterns, Tanomogi and the other conspirators consider the machine to be the true version of Katsumi, and thus take the machine's orders over the real doctor's! As the machine has looked into the future and predicted a new ice age, it deems the Aquans the best choice for mankind's survival. When the real Katsumi refuses to go along with this plan, the machine orders him to be terminated.

OVERVIEW: Kobo Abe's *Inter Ice Age 4* has been described by some as the first full-length Japanese science fiction novel. It was published July 5, 1959 by Kodansha. Before that, in March of 1958, it was serialized in *Sekai Magazine*. Abe's first movie adaptation was *Pitfall* (1962) which was followed by *The*

23

Woman in the Dunes (1964) which was very well received. Having found great success in the field of fantastical films, in 1965, Toho secured the screen rights to *Inter Ice Age 4*. The screenplay was written at a condominium in Shiraki Ranch at Sengaki Falls by Abe himself. The film's proposed director was to be Hiromichi Horikawa, second unit director on such Kurosawa classics as *Seven Samurai* (1954) and *Throne of Blood* (1957). Horikawa was quoted as saying, "I was obsessed with making this work into a movie." What exactly killed *Inter Ice Age 4* is unknown, as Toho was experiencing smooth sailing for the most part in 1965. It is presumable that perhaps the needed effects work and copious underwater filming is what led to the film's cancellation.

Many of the book's more fantastic scenes focus on underwater farms where livestock like cows and pigs have been genetically modified to have gills. Along with them are the Aquans, a group of humans created from "aborted" fetuses that the scientists manipulate into having gills. However, the Aquans are certainly not grotesque gill-men, but appear to be normal humans with gills. Their only other strange feature is that they never blink being underwater.

Though this author has never seen the script, he has read the English translation of the novel done by Dale Saunders. It was published in 1970 by the publisher Alfred Knopf out of New York. Since author Abe wrote the movie script it is presumable it follows the novel fairly closely. Though one can't say how the novel would have translated on screen, it makes for an intriguing read that keeps the reader guessing. For instance, when Katsumi begins following a random stranger to test out his predictive machine on and it leads to a conspiracy involving gilled-humans it seems like too much of a coincidence. Or rather, from a narrative standpoint it seems odd that a story seemingly about a super computer would take a turn into Gill Man territory. As it turns out, the coincidence is no coincidence at all, and Katsumi was very subtly led by his assistant Tanomogi into following the "stranger". As the story progresses, we learn that Tanomogi actually murdered the man on Katsumi's own instructions!

Over the course of the story, Katsumi receives mysterious, threatening phone calls at his home warning him not to delve too deeply into the conspiracy. Eventually it becomes evident that the voice is remarkably Katsumi's own! This isn't a voice from the future though, but a voice that can predict the future belonging to the machine. As it turns out, Tanomogi input the professor's thought patterns into the machine creating a mechanical clone of his brain. The machine is referred to as a smarter, more ideal version of Katsumi, and has been orchestrating all the events in the story since it came online. Ironically, Katsumi's own staff begins to follow the orders of the machine over his own, considering the machine a better, more perfected version of Katsumi's own mind! When the machine predicts that Katsumi will not go along with the Aquan plot, it suggests that they kill him and they have no trouble obliging. However, they do at least try to make Katsumi see the future so that he may change his mind.

The climax of the book has Katsumi watching a simulated prediction of the future. This is where Eiji Tsuburaya would have excelled, as it features the sinking of Japan and the rest of the world under the rising oceans. One scene in the book has a tidal wave decimating parts of Japan while beneath the waves, the Aquans go peacefully about their day—not even noting the turmoil above them. The book delves so deeply into the future that eventually the Aquans, initially slaves of sorts, transition into the true rulers of the earth.

Eventually, normal human society disappears altogether. The final sequence has Katsumi watching a simulation of a young Aquan man who longs to visit the surface—even if it costs him his life. The young Aquan manages to make his way to a small island where he crawls ashore and soon dies. The small island is soon engulfed by the sea, and the film ends as Katsumi seems to view the dead Aquan as a kindred spirit in that both of them refuse to accept the future. Katsumi sits in wait for his killer, listening to his footsteps just outside the door, and the novel ends. Perhaps this was Abe's way of showing that the future isn't certain, and we the reader will never know Katsumi's fate even though all signs point to him being murdered.

The bleak future shock script would have been ahead of its time for cinemas in 1966 and would have predated *Planet of the Apes* (1968) as one of the great sci-fi shockers. Tsuburaya would have also had his hands full if the script was adapted faithfully from the book. For instance, there is a lengthy scene where the doctors tour the testing facility and are introduced to underwater cows, dogs and pigs among other creatures. There are also two overgrown fly larvae kept in a cage. While Tsuburaya always excelled at creating made-up kaiju, sometimes his recreations of real life animals were lacking. Here Tsuburaya would have had to create gilled pigs and cows. Had these sequences been created poorly it would have greatly undermined the story's serious tone. And, as stated earlier, perhaps it was these effects concerns that cancelled the production, though no official reason has ever been stated.

"The Radioactive King of the Monsters!" "The Universe-Guarding Friend to Children!" "The Mightiest Moth in All Creation!" You won't find them here. No, this is not a collection reviewing the same old giant monster movies that we've all seen covered countless times already. This book is for those who've already watched those, and are looking for a new fix, outside of those familiar franchise behemoths. Here you'll find information on the more esoteric kaiju cinema experience: quirky parodies (such as BIG MAN JAPAN and ULTRAMAN ZEARTH), animated features (like CYBORG 009: WAR OF THE MONSTERS), Taiwanese fantasy flicks (e.g. KING OF SNAKE and its better-known Hong Kong edition, THUNDER OF GIGANTIC SERPENT), low-budget indie pictures (including MONSTER MOVIE G and OROCHI STRIKES AGAIN), TV miniseries (for example, MOONLIGHT MASK: MAMMOTH KONG or IRON ARMOR MIKAZUKI), and more. There's a lot to enjoy, so come take a walk down the road less trampled.

Available on AMAZON.COM
for only $19.99

THE LOST FILMS FANZINE PRESENTS MOVIE MILESTONES #3

GENOCIDE

Release Date: November 09, 1968 Japanese Title: *Great Insect War* (Japan) *War of the Insects* (U.S.) *The Destroying Invasion* (Spain) *The Hallucinating End of Humanity* (Italy) *Death Opens His Wings* (Greece) *Genocide - The Killer Bees Attack* (Germany)

DIRECTED BY: Kazui Nihonmatsu SPECIAL EFFECTS BY: Keiji Kawakami & Shun Suganuma SCREENPLAY BY: Susumu Takaku MUSIC BY: Shunsuke Kikuchi CAST: Yusuke Kawazu (Joji), Keisuke Sonoi (Yoshito), Emi Shindo (Yukari), Reiko Hitomi (Junko), Kathy Horan (Annabel), Chico Roland (Charlie)

Shochiku GrandScope, Eastmancolor, 84 Minutes

SYNOPSIS A U.S. Air Force plane carrying a hydrogen bomb on the way to Vietnam is attacked by a swarm of poisonous insects and crashes in the waters near Japan's southernmost islands. As the U.S. military searches for the missing bomb and mysterious insect attacks mount, it is learned the killer bees are being controlled by a woman named Annabel. A biologist who survived the Nazi holocaust, Annabel is using the insects to inflict genocide on the world. Annabel reveals that the insects of the world have decided that if mankind explodes one more atomic weapon, they will annihilate man. When this plot is uncovered by scientist Joji, he kills Annabel by trapping her in a room with her deadly bees who sting her to death. As the insects overtake the islands, the U.S. Air Force decides the best way to solve all of their problems is to detonate the H-Bomb, in effect killing the insects and also ensuring the H-Bomb doesn't fall into enemy hands. After the bomb is detonated, the insects attack and cause the plane to explode, killing everyone on board. Yukari, Joji's pregnant girlfriend and lone survivor, watches in a rowboat and begins to pray as mankind's last day has come...

OVERVIEW: Directed by the same man that gave the world the awful *The X From Outer Space* the previous year, Kazui Nihonmatsu does a much better job on this insect-themed horror film written by Susumu Takaku (*Goke, Body Snatcher from Hell*). The film was shot on location on Hachijo Island often using real insects. In fact, in one scene, a real bee bites lead actor Yusuke Kawazu.

Scenes of the insects in action brought to life via animated swarms (and in the case of close-ups, real bees) aren't ter-

GENOCIDE © 1968 SHICHOKU CO., LTD.

ribly interesting from a special effects perspective. The first occurs when a swarm chokes the engines of the air force plane carrying the H-Bomb. More interesting than the film's insects is its use of apocalyptic imagery as the film both opens and closes with the detonation of hydrogen bombs. In the case of the film's opening the bomb is just stock footage, but in the case of the ending, the weapon is remotely detonated by the air force to destroy both the insects and the bomb. One of the airmen tries to stop the detonation aboard a military aircraft, but when his attempt proves futile and the bomb detonates anyways (blown by a shot commander who pettily presses the button as he dies), he shoots himself in the head. Moments later, another swarm of insect descends upon the plane, choking the engines and destroying it while at the same time showing the bomb didn't take care of the bugs after all.

What is most perplexing about the film is that it was made the same year as and amounts to little more than a remake of *Goke* with insects instead of aliens. The film has a slightly different story, but it follows the exact same beats and has more or less the exact same ending: everybody dies (other than Yukari in her boat) and the world ends (or will end). Shunsuke Kikuchi's score could even be mistaken for outtakes from *Goke*.

Released on a double bill with *The Living Skeleton* in Japan, *Genocide* ended up being the last of Shochiku's horror films as the studio switched gears to begin producing the family friendly (and very long running) Tora-san series. *Genocide* also saw limited release in America under the title *War of the Insects* through Shochiku Films of America in 1969.

JAPAN SINKS!!!

In 1964, novelist Sakyo Komatsu began work on his epic novel *Submersion of Japan*, which was finally completed and published on March 20, 1973 by Kobunsha Kappa in two volumes. The first print run was a smash success selling over 3 million copies, raking in ¥120,000,000.

As always, there are alternating accounts of when and where Toho acquired the film rights to the book. One account states that Tomoyuki Tanaka had optioned it for film even before it was published, but the book *Japan Sinks 1973 Complete Documentation* would make it seem Tanaka read it the very day it was published and called Komatsu on the phone that evening! In an interview with *Science Fiction Studies*, Sakyo Komatsu explained that he felt a great deal of gratitude towards Toho for their kind treat-ment of him in the early 1960s when he was first starting out. "I felt so obligated that in 1973 when we were discussing a film version of *Japan Sinks*, I gave them the movie rights with almost no conditions. I think they paid 1.5 million yen."

Toho's intent to produce the film was announced in newspapers on May 24th with an expected start date in September. The plan at the time was to complete filming by January and have the film out in March of 1974. Also, one of the proposed directors was none other than Akira Kurosawa himself. At some point, Toho decided to make the film a New Year's release for that December instead, and also increased the film's budget in the process—the equivalent of $3 million, then a nearly unheard of cost for a Japanese feature! On June 18th, Shiro Moritani was announced as the chosen director and casting also began with popular *Kamen Rider* star Hiroshi Fujioka cast as Onodera. Despite author Komatsu's wishes to have Kaoru Yumi cast as Reiko, Ayumi Ishida got the part instead. Renowned actor Tetsuro Tamba (best known in the west for his role as Tiger Tanaka in *You Only Live Twice*) was cast as the Prime Minister Yamamoto. Author Komatsu would even cameo in an early scene between Onodera and Yoshimura, and Haruo Nakajima, recently retired from playing Godzilla, has a cameo as the Prime Minister's chauffeur.

Behind the scenes, the film featured a great deal of future talent that would one day go on to work on the Heisei and Millennium Godzilla movies. Assisting Teruyoshi Nakano with special effects was Koichi Kawakita (the Heisei Godzilla series special effects director) and Eiichi Asada (special effects director on the last two Millennium Godzilla films). As assistant director was Koji Hashimoto, who

would himself helm a Komatsu disaster film of his own, *Sayonara Jupiter*, after Moritani's passing.

To give their film adaptation as much realism as possible, several authorities actually consulted on the film, among them geophysics expert Professor Hitoshi Takeuchi, seismic engineering professor Yorihiko Osaki, oceanography expert Professor Noriyuki Nasu, and volcanologist Akira Suwa, director of the Meteorological and Earthquake Research Institute. The film went through four script drafts in all.

DAIEI'S JAPAN SINKS! Before Sakyo Komatsu could publish his book, SUBMERSION OF JAPAN, and before Toho could adapt it for film, Daiei almost adapted the concept for screens. The sequence of events given by Japanese website cyberkids1954 states that in early 1971, Daiei was toying with making a film about the Great Tokyo Earthquake. Then in the fall of 1971, Daiei caught wind of Sakyo Komatsu's novel and wanted to adapt it. Prematurely, or without a written agreement with Sakyo Komatsu, Daiei President Masaichi Nagata announced that the company would produce THE SINKING OF THE JAPANESE ARCHIPELAGO. Also announced alongside of this film was GAMERA VS. TWO HEADED MONSTER W. Daiei declared its official bankruptcy in December of 1971 (though it had been bankrupt since 1970), and neither film was made.

THE LOST FILMS FANZINE PRESENTS MOVIE MILESTONES #3

SUBMERSION OF JAPAN

Release Date: December 29, 1973
Alternate Titles:
Tidal Wave (U.S.) *Panic Over Tokyo* (Germany) *S.O.S. Earth Drops* (Sweden) *Death of the Rising Sun* (Portugal) *Destruction of Japan* (Poland) *Planet Earth: Year Zero* (Italy) *Destruction Came from the Bottom of the Ocean* (Greece)

DIRECTED BY: Shiro Moritani SPECIAL EFFECTS BY: Teruyoshi Nakano SCREENPLAY BY: Shinobu Hashimoto MUSIC BY: Masaru Sato CAST: Hiroshi Fujioka (Toshio Onodera), Tetsuro Tamba (Prime Minister Yamamoto), Ayumi Ishida (Reiko), Keiji Kobayashi (Dr. Tadokoro), Shogo Shimada (Prince Watari), Nobuo Nakamura (Australian Ambassador), Andrew Hughes (Australian Prime Minister)

Panavision, Eastmancolor, 140 Minutes

SYNOPSIS When an island mysteriously sinks into the ocean overnight, Dr. Tadokoro is sent to investigate. In a submarine piloted by Onodera, Tadokoro makes a startling discovery in the Japan Trench. The doctor hypothesis that within a matter of years Japan will sink into the ocean. However, it becomes apparent the submersion will happen much sooner than that when an earthquake devastates Kanto, killing millions. Preparations are made to evacuate as many Japanese to other nations as possible. As Japan continues to sink into the sea, Dr. Tadokoro decides to die with the nation he loves, while Onodera searches for his missing fiancé, Reiko, in an unknown country (likely Russia).

OVERVIEW: The production values on this film are incredibly high when compared to the Godzilla films of the same era, and features a cast of superstars such as Tetsuro Tamba as the Prime Minister and Hiroshi Fujioka as Onodera. Kenji Kobayashi gives an excellent performance as Dr. Tadokoro, the tortured scientist who first learns that Japan is doomed to sink into the ocean. The scene where he tries to convey the gravity of this fact to his colleague is one of the thespian's highlights of the film. Another excellent scene occurs when Onodera, sworn to silence by the government, walks down a crowded street in Osaka tormented by the fact he can't warn his fellow countrymen as to Japan's fate.

The film is easily the crown jewel of special effects director Teruyoshi Nakano's works. One of the highlights is certainly the earthquake that decimates Kanto. It is truly horrific as people catch fire and others are graphically injured by showering shards of glass that rain down on them from a skyscraper. In one scene, an old man fearfully frets about the fires that started in the Kanto earthquake of 1923 only to be swallowed up by a massive wall of water. The aftermath of this scene is also impressive, as helicopters try to put out fires in the decimated city. The rest of the destruction is limited mostly to urban areas and though it is fascinating to watch for fans of miniature effects, the Kanto earthquake remains the film's best scene. But *Submersion of Japan* is not merely an effects film; it's a solid disaster movie reminiscent of American cinema from the time like *Earthquake* (which this film precedes, by the way). Actually, it could be said this film surpasses many of the American-made disaster films in terms of story, atmosphere, special effects, and cinematography. A shot of Onodera running into the sun, obscured by volcanic ash, is particularly outstanding especially because it was created with practical effects. Somewhat misplaced is Sato's score which lacks the gravity of Ifukube's works. While it is by no means a bad score (in fact, it's quite poignant), it simply isn't downbeat enough most of the time, and fans of the Godzilla series will find sections reminiscent of *Godzilla vs. Mechagodzilla* which Sato would score the next year.

The merits of the film's last act are debatable. It is somewhat flawed in that it totally loses track of Onodera. However, this could have been the intent of director Shiro Moritani as Onodera has himself lost track of his lover Reiko and many of Japan's citizens are being scattered across the globe. And although the last act is peppered with various scenes of destruction, it lacks a final set-piece to truly cap-off the film. Instead, the climax is an emotional one as the Prime Minister has one last meeting with Dr. Tadokoro, who delivers a touching eulogy of sorts to Japan. The final scene shows both Onodera and Reiko inside trains on different sides of the world, letting the audience leave the film wondering if ever the two shall meet again.

Released in late December of 1973, *Submersion of Japan* garnered 8.8 million admissions and became the highest grossing Japanese-made film of the 1970s and would influence Toho's output for years to come. Part of the reason why the film was so popular was because it perfectly captured the fears of the Japanese people. Author Stuart Galbraith summarized it best in his book *Japanese Science Fiction, Fantasy, and Horror Films* where he wrote, "it dramatized one of the most innate fears among Japanese citizens: the disastrous annihilation, natural or otherwise, of their vulnerable nation."

THE BOOK VS. THE MOVIE:

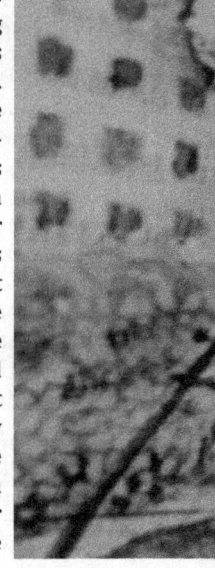

As stated earlier, Sakyo Komatsu began work on the novel all the way back in 1964. "Let me discuss why I wrote that novel," Komatsu told Brett Homenick in *G-Fan* magazine #80:

I started to write *Nippon Chinbotsu* in 1964, and it took 9 years to complete. Until 15th of August 1945, when the Showa Emperor officially declared the end of the war to the Japanese nation, all the Japanese, especially a teenager like me, believed in governmental slogans such as "honorable death for all hundred million Japanese nations" or "decisive battle is when Americans landed on mainland Japan." We all made up our mind for the coming death. However, once the war was over, Japanese overcame the consequence of defeat so easily, and by the 1960s, people were happy about the rapid economical growth of the country. When I saw those circumstances, I wanted to reconsider the meaning of what "Japan" is and what "Japanese" are. That is why I wrote *Nippon Chinbotsu*. [pp.56]

Of the film adaptation, Komatsu later said, "I was quite surprised when Toho had completed the film just after the book was published. The movie was quite faithful to the original story, and I was quite satisfied." That said, there are naturally plenty of differences between the novel, the four scripts, and the finished film.

The book begins with Onodera walking through a sweaty mass of people on the street. He is on his way to take the train to his next assignment when he has a chance meeting with Rokuro Go, a worker on the Super Express Line—a character that didn't make it into the movie. The two share a beer on the train and Onodera tells him about the island that recently sank. The film, on the other hand, begins with Onodera looking over the *Wadatsumi*, where

SCRIPTING JAPAN SINKS

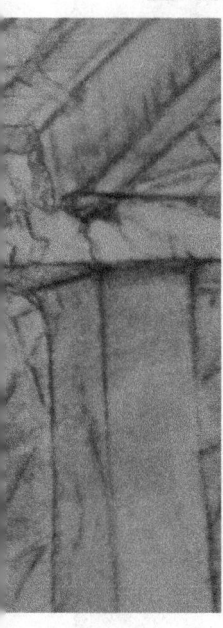

he is soon introduced to Dr. Tadokoro—described in the book as a portly man, not the dignified figure cut by actor Keiji Kobayashi in the film.

Another significant scene in the book had Onodera and the others witnessing a volcanic eruption at sea while on the way to their diving point. This sequence was included in the first draft of the script and was removed with rewrites. In another scene from the book, Onodera and the crew also receive testimony from the Japanese and Polynesian fishermen who were on the island when it sunk. Naturally, the movie has to condense the action and there are only two trips down below in the *Wadatsumi* but in the book, there are three. In one trip, the men see a quasi-kaiju: a 100-foot long stingray!

One of the bigger subplots in the book and the movie has Onodera's boss Yoshimura setting him up with a wealthy heiress, Reiko Abe, in the hopes that he can then promote Onodera within the company. In the novel, Yoshimura takes Onodera to a club and informs him of these plans while in the movie, he simply does so in his office. Also at the club, Onodera meets a hostess named Mako. Though this character wasn't included in the film, she has a significant impact on the book's final scene. After informing him of his plans, Yoshimura drives Onodera to Reiko's house to meet her. In the movie, this also happens and once we see Yoshimura pull up to the house, we immediately cut to Reiko and Onodera having a solo dinner getting to know one another.

In the book, Reiko is having a party. Onodera mingles with various industrial types, one of which wants to create an underwater amusement park. In the book and movie alike, Reiko and Onodera go off alone for a swim in the ocean where Reiko reveals she knows of Yoshimura's plan. The two have a civil but somewhat awkward conversation

THE LOST FILMS FANZINE PRESENTS MOVIE MILESTONES #3

Above: Yuki (Isao Natsuyagi), Onodera (Hiroshi Fujioka) and Tadokoro (Keiji Kobayashi) in the WADATSUMI. Opposite Page: Onodera and Reiko (Ayumi Ishida). SUBMERSION OF JAPAN © 1973 TOHO CO., LTD.

but Reiko is actually interested in Onodera. In the book, it is stated that the two make love on the beach while the film only hints at this. In the book, as they lay on the beach, Onodera hears a radio report on the death of his friend Go, an apparent suicide because of his failure working on the Super Express line. After this revelation, the earthquake occurs. Onodera takes the party guests back to Tokyo via hovercraft in Sagami Bay. Onodera soon receives a phone call from Dr. Tadokoro requesting he come to his lab immediately. Furthermore, Tadokoro is funded by a mysterious, unseen group called The Church of the Seven Seas. In the film, the BAC World Oceanic Foundation is his sponsor.

Another significant scene exclusive to the book has Onodera enduring an earthquake in Kyoto at Go's funeral. From this point forward, the book and movie are quite similar up to the great Tokyo earthquake. In the book, the earthquake scene is told through the eyes of a character that only appears in the book, Yamazaki. Tadokoro and Onodera's ship then sails into Tokyo to help with rescue efforts in the water, something that doesn't happen in the film. The movie deals more with the aftermath of the earthquake while the book jumps ahead in time. As investigations into the Japan Trench continue, the book has an exciting scene not in the movie where Onodera is picked up from his research ship after doing a dive in unstable volcanic waters. While flying above the ship, a character named Katoaka informs Onodera that a submarine, likely from a foreign power, is spying on them (Japan's sinking has not yet been made public).

When Dr. Tadokoro confirms Japan's impending doom aboard the ship he states, "Even a child can figure out what will happen next." That line was scripted to take place inside the ship's control room in the final draft. During shooting, they decided the scene would work better on the deck. The movie also has Dr. Tadokoro prematurely release the dreadful news on live TV. When a reporter makes light of the situation, Tadokoro even attacks him! The scientist is labeled a quack and not everyone takes his prediction seriously. No such thing happens in the book.

After Onodera reconnects with Reiko, both plan to leave Japan for Switzerland. However, they are separated when Mt. Fuji erupts. In the book, Reiko disappears after her phone call to Onodera and for all we know, she may have died. In one draft of the script, the last we see of Reiko is her fainting during the Mt. Fuji eruption and there is no reveal that she is still alive in the final scene. Later drafts inserted Reiko into the tsunami scene where she is seen overlooking the shore and about to board a boat bound illegally for Korea. Onodera trying to warn the people going out to sea at the fishing port is not in the book either nor was it in early script drafts.

Though the movie has a montage of Onodera's efforts to rescue as many Japanese as possible, the book has a notable scene not in the film. Onodera and his chopper crew come across some stranded hikers who wish to climb the Japanese Alps one last time before they sink. Onodera gives up his spot on the chopper so that as many as possible can be flown to safety. Among the hikers who must stay are Mako, the hostess from earlier in the book. An eruption occurs, and this is the last we see of Onodera until the last few pages of the book...

The film ends with Dr. Tadokoro and Prime Minister Yamamoto sharing a lengthy talk about why Tadokoro wishes to die with Japan rather than be saved. It occurs right outside of Prince Watari's home after he has passed. In the book, the Prime Minister—who doesn't have the presence that actor Tetsuro Tamba brings to the onscreen character—has already evacuated. Instead, this scene takes place between Tadokoro and Watari, simply known as "the old man" in the book. Watari compares the Japanese to infants who are losing their mother. In the movie, this dialogue is given to Tadokoro in his talk to the Prime Minister. This section of the book, before the old man dies, also

includes one of Komatsu's most lamented deleted scenes. As the old man's youthful servant, Hanai, tells him that she wishes to stay by his side, he begs her to leave and have a life of her own. When he insists that she also change clothes for her journey, he asks if he may see her naked body and she obliges. "I wanted that in the movie, even if they had to film it from behind," Komatsu told *Science Fiction Studies*.

The movie famously ends with Reiko and Onodera on different trains, possibly on different sides of the world or even rolling past one another. This ending wasn't given to the film until late in the game and it's certainly not how the book ends. The book has something of a surprise ending, albeit an unhappy one. Onodera wakes up on what he thinks is a ship. He is in a foggy state of mind and the girl attending to him reminds him that she is his wife. We, as the reader, wonder if this is Reiko that he's finally been reunited with. Onodera asks her several times if Japan has sunk and to look out the port window and see. In the last two paragraphs, Komatsu reveals Onodera's fate: he's not on a ship with Reiko. He's on a train in Siberia with Mako, whom he has apparently married. We never learn what happened to Reiko and the book ends.

Page Opposite: Onodera and Reiko share a kiss on the beach (top); foreign release poster (bottom). Left: Before SUBMERSION OF JAPAN, SPFX director Teruyoshi Nakano was best known for the Godzilla series (seen here on the set of 1973's GODZILLA VS. MEGALON); This Page and Following: various behind the scenes stills from SUBMERSION OF JAPAN. SUBMERSION OF JAPAN/GODZILLA VS. MEGALON ©

THE LOST FILMS FANZINE PRESENTS MOVIE MILESTONES #3

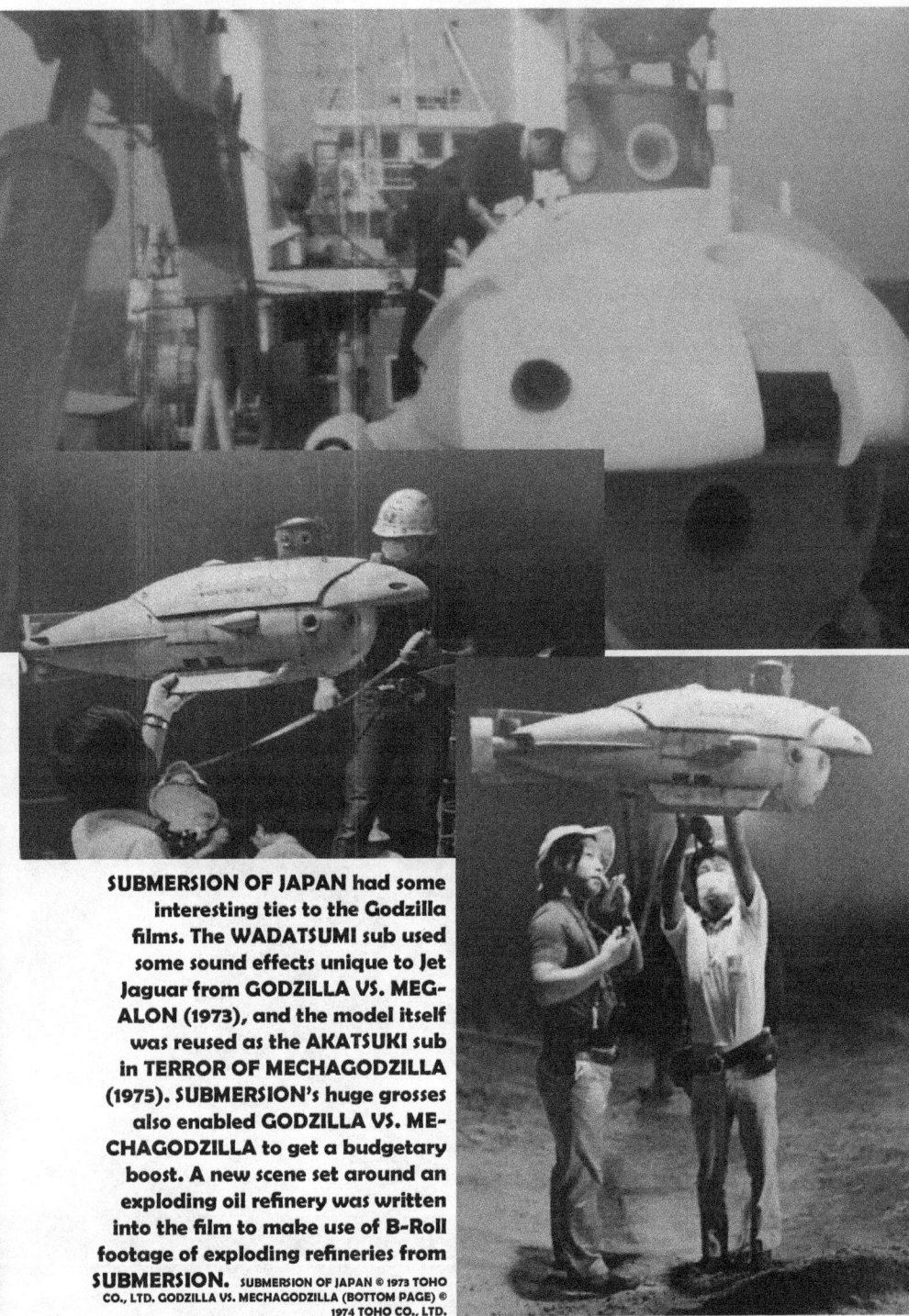

SUBMERSION OF JAPAN had some interesting ties to the Godzilla films. The **WADATSUMI** sub used some sound effects unique to Jet Jaguar from **GODZILLA VS. MEGALON** (1973), and the model itself was reused as the **AKATSUKI** sub in **TERROR OF MECHAGODZILLA** (1975). **SUBMERSION**'s huge grosses also enabled **GODZILLA VS. MECHAGODZILLA** to get a budgetary boost. A new scene set around an exploding oil refinery was written into the film to make use of B-Roll footage of exploding refineries from **SUBMERSION**. SUBMERSION OF JAPAN © 1973 TOHO CO., LTD. GODZILLA VS. MECHAGODZILLA (BOTTOM PAGE) © 1974 TOHO CO., LTD.

THE LOST FILMS FANZINE PRESENTS MOVIE MILESTONES #3

39

JAPAN SINKS IN AMERICA:

TIDAL WAVE

JAPAN/U.S.
Submersion of Japan/Tidal Wave
December 29, 1973/May, 1975
143 minutes/80 minutes
Cut Footage: 71 minutes
Added Scenes: 8 minutes
DIRECTOR: Shiro Moritani/
Andrew Mayer
PRODUCER: Tomoyuki Tanaka,
Osamu Tanaka/Roger Corman
WRITER: Shinobu Hashimoto & Sakyo
Komatsu (novel)/Andrew Mayer
ADDED CAST: Lorne Greene (Richards), John Fujioka (Narita), Rhonda
Leigh Hopkins (Fran)

The following is a special comparison between SUBMERSION OF JAPAN and TIDAL WAVE (it is a sample chapter of the yet-to-be-published book EDITING JAPANESE MONSTERS, due out later in 2021). Note that footage, music, and alterations unique to both versions are emboldened.

When American audiences saw *Tidal Wave* in 1975 they probably thought it was an "inferior Japanese rip-off" of popular American disaster films such as *Earthquake* and *The Towering Inferno* (both 1974) when it in fact preceded them in Japan. Roger Corman's New World Pictures saw the potential in 1973's *Submersion of Japan* as a disaster movie. As earthquakes had already been emphasized in the aforementioned *Earthquake*, Corman decided to retitle the film *Tidal Wave* as he probably felt a disaster movie with Japan's name in the title might turn away U.S. audiences. In a further attempt to make the film more appealing to westerners, Corman brought in a famous Western star, *Bonanza's* Lorne Greene, to anchor new footage exclusive to the U.S. version.

Filming of the new footage was completed in only two—possibly three—days. The process was incredibly simple. New director Andrew Mayer wrote 20 pages of dialogue and then Corman rented out a hotel suite for the weekend—therefor no sets had to be built. Cameraman Eric Saarinen recalled the nature of the scenes to Brett Homenick in *G-Fan* #79 stating that, "It was just dialogue, you know, and it was stuff you'd cut back and forth from...from the Japanese [cast] somewhere else or to the wave or whatever...there was a sort of revolving door of fairly well-known actors that would come in and take different parts of generals, or, you know,

MAKING A TIDAL WAVE

the American interests." Of Greene, Saarinen said, "Lorne Greene was a total professional, and very well liked amongst the small crew." Saarinen also recalled how the hotel rooms were re-dressed to become various "war rooms and embassies". He remarked that it looked somewhat ludicrous to have a giant panoramic camera (the aspect ratios had to match the Japanese footage) on such small sets with skeleton crews of six to eight men. "It was kind of a joke filming these very small sets with the huge camera."

Overall, only eight minutes of new footage was integrated into the film while over one hour's worth of footage was cut! Komatsu was aware of this adaptation too and told Brett Homenick in *G-Fan* that, "I know that the movie was heavily re-edited and made into a disaster movie and released in U.S. with the title of *Tidal Wave*. However, the original story depicts the natural and calamity environments of Japan and the Japanese way of thinking which is based on such environment."

This author saw *Submersion of Japan*, a fine film, before *Tidal Wave*. As such, I always puzzled at Roger Ebert's rather nasty review of the film. After having seen *Tidal Wave*, I can see why Ebert reviewed the film thusly:

Bad movies are really getting awful these days. It seems like only yesterday we were savoring bombs like "The Vengeance of She" and "Godzilla vs. the Smog Monster" movies so terrible they achieved a sort of greatness. Movies in which there were lines like "I have waited 3,000 years for this day" and newspaper reporters who let their voices trail off at the end of declarations like: "But, doctor, if your predictions are correct, this means the end of civilization on Earth..."

I was hoping 'Tidal Wave" would be a movie like that. When the publicity photographs arrived in the mail a few weeks ago, I was heartened by the sight of the staples holding together the cardboard skyscrapers: Here was a movie with real lack of promise! It even looked like a good bet to outflank "King Kong vs. Godzilla." (What happened in that one, as I recall, is that King Kong lost and is currently trying to promote a bout with the Smog Monster, to establish himself as a contender once again.) But "Tidal Wave" let me down. It is purely and simply a wretched failure, a feeble attempt to paste together inept special effects (filmed in Japan) and Lorne Greene (filmed in America to his everlasting regret, I'll bet).

Ebert concluded his review by writing, "The movie never ends, but if you wait long enough it gets to a point where it's over." Had Ebert seen the original *Submersion of Japan*, his opinion may have been different. In addition to cutting away many character scenes and themes, the deadpan dubbing in *Tidal Wave* is so awful it's no wonder why Ebert drubbed the film so badly. Ultimately, the dubbing chips away the film's dignity and credibility because the performances are that bad. Arguably Corman would have been better off spending some money on better dubbing rather than the new hotelroom shot Lorne Greene scenes.

To get to the differences, *Submersion of Japan* begins with the **Toho Logo followed by a blue title card that reads "A Toho Movie Inc. and a Toho Vision Inc. Co-production".** This is followed by a large earth prop against a white background which illustrates the concept of continental drift over millions of years. There is no narration, just Japanese slates identifying the time period (or passage of years in the millions) each time the continents change. As we focus on the development of Ja-

THE LOST FILMS FANZINE PRESENTS MOVIE MILESTONES #3

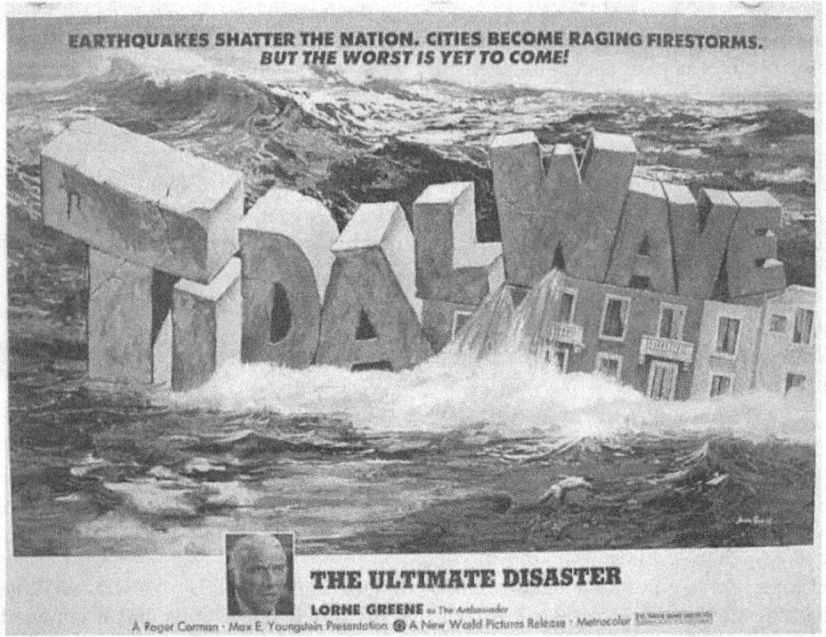

pan some fog begins to obscure the screen and **the title comes onscreen in bold red letters.** Before the rest of the credits roll, **we hear the roar of a bullet train as we fade into an image of one racing across the countryside. The credits then display over various scenes including, in this order, a Japanese festival, a horse race, a baseball game, and then various scenes showing large crowds of Japanese,** such as rows of cars and beach goers.

Tidal Wave begins with **the New World Logo set to new music**, not from Masaru Sato, followed by **a black title card that reads in simple, yellow letters, "Lorne Greene in" which is followed by the title, "Tidal Wave", and then the full cast and crew credits.** The new music isn't bad at all, and is more ominous than the opening, **upbeat tune composed by Sato** (he ironically gets the sole credit on the music even though the music currently playing is not his own, but nor is his score replaced again throughout the rest of *Tidal Wave*). We then cut to the earth diagram footage. It is **sped up and truncated and includes narration by Lorne Greene explaining continental drift and the formation of Japan.** At the point that the title is inserted in the Japanese version we cut to a shot of Misaki Port also present in the original version, but **shortened** in *Tidal Wave* and minus the **Japanese slates** identifying it as Misaki Port.

In both versions' first major scene, Dr. Tadokoro (Keiju Kobayashi) arrives at the ship where he meets Onodera (Hiroshi Fujioka), pilot of the submersible *Wadatsumi*, who will pilot him to the sea bottom to investigate an island that recently sank. However, via the English dub, **Dr. Tadokoro becomes "Mr. Tanaka" and Onodera becomes "Onoda"** in *Tidal Wave*. Otherwise the scene is more or less the same with a few differences in dialogue and is shortened by all of around ten seconds only. As this scene ends, the Japanese version cuts to **a shot of the boat from behind, then does a wipe transition** into a shot of the ship from the side.

Tidal Wave cuts straight to the shot of the ship from the side, skipping the rear view shot. The Japanese version of this shot has **signage identifying the location as being north of the Ogasawara Islands** which the U.S. version removes.

As Tadokoro enters the sub while Onodera and a coworker watch, **the U.S. dub adds in some animosity between "Tanaka" and "Onoda", who jokes about the old man as he slips inside the sub.** The underwater diving scene in the *Wadatsumi* appears to be uncut and unaltered aside from the dub. The following meeting scene back on the ship, discussing the sunken island, is condensed greatly with **a few additional shots of the sunken island (and discussion regarding it)** removed. The ending of the scene is also chopped off. In *Submersion of Japan* Dr. Tadokoro asks Onodera if it's possible to dive to the bottom of the Japan Trench tomorrow, and Onodera affirms that they can. Soon a crewman enters and informs the men that abnormal activity has been detected near the Boso and Ogasawara trenches.

In *Tidal Wave*, the end of this scene—where "Tanaka" announces they need to do more research—jumps into *Submersion of Japan's* love story between Onodera and Reiko Abe (Ayumi Ishida), a wealthy heiress whom Onodera's boss wants him to marry. In effect, *Tidal Wave* skips over a great many scenes that preceded Onodera and Reiko's first meeting, including the introductory scene of Prime Minister Yamamoto (Tetsuro Tamba). In the scene, **Yamamoto arrives at his private home. There, in his study, he looks at a map of the Japan Trench while dialogue (meant to be a replay of something Yamamoto heard earlier) plays detailing what Yamamoto knows about the current situation. From here we cut to a scene between Onodera and his boss, Yoshimura (Shigeru Kôyama). While standing before Yoshimura's desk, Onodera gets a call from an exasperated Dr. Tadokoro asking if it would be possible to charter the *Wadatsumi* ASAP to continue his investigation of the Japan Trench. When Onodera informs him the sub is rented out for the duration of the next year Tadokoro becomes angry and hangs up. The scene continues with Yoshimura breaching the subject of Onodera's future with him, asking him if he plans to marry soon.**

In the next scene, **Yoshimura drives Onodera to Hayama to meet Reiko, whom Yoshimura wants to connect Onodera with. As Yoshimura pulls into Reiko's driveway the scene fades away** to the scene present in *Tidal Wave*, where Reiko opens a blind. As she and Onodera share a drink over dinner, **the U.S. version dubs in a line about Reiko's father being impressed with Onodera's diving work.** This isn't mentioned in the Japanese version of the scene, which is slightly extended. In the original scene **both acknowledge that Reiko's father and Onodera's boss are trying to force a marriage out of convenience.** In *Submersion of Japan*, we get a better idea of why they want the two to be wed. **Reiko's father owns several islands, near which Onodera had explored the sea floor to see if they had ore for mining**. However, in *Tidal Wave*, without the preceding scene, for all we know Reiko and Onodera have met before, and there is no indication that this is their very first meeting. The *Tidal Wave* dub awkwardly ends the scene by having **Reiko tell Onoda, "Show me your ocean, I want to feel it."** The Japanese version isn't so corny, and **Reiko simply invites Onodera to go swimming.**

However, to their credit, the U.S. editors shortened the scene without butchering the soundtrack—at least until the very end. **The soundtrack is altered** in one unfortunate way due to the shortening of the scene. When *Sub-*

THE LOST FILMS FANZINE PRESENTS MOVIE MILESTONES #3

Onodera (Hiroshi Fujioka) and Reiko (Ayumi Ishida) witnessing the eruption of Mt. Amagi. SUBMERSION OF JAPAN © 1973 TOHO CO., LTD.

mersion of Japan cuts to the surf (after Reiko asks Onodera to go swimming) **the music becomes passionate** rather than gloomy. In Tidal Wave, **we cut to the surf while the gloomy music still plays**, and this goes on as Reiko and Onodera are seen kissing which is rather inappropriate. (The gloomy music had played as Onodera described the disturbing underwater current he witnessed with Dr. Tadokoro in the original version of the scene.) The passionate note doesn't kick in until a few moments later as the two now lie on the beach, presumably after more than just a kiss has happened. Once again, Tidal Wave's dialogue is cringe worthy.

Reiko: Your wet body feels so good.
Onoda: Yes.
Reiko: Wet and safe and warm.

Onoda: Just like yours.
Reiko: Hold me tight!

The Japanese dialogue actually has something to say to move the plot forward. It's also bit more obvious the two have just made love as Reiko asks him again about marriage. Though this dialogue may not look great on paper alone, it's well acted.

Reiko: You will get married sooner or later?
Onodera: Yeah.
Reiko: Why? What for?
Onodera: [pause] To have a baby?
Reiko: Hey...Hold me.

In both versions Mt. Amagi erupts and in Tidal Wave's continuity we cut straight to a scene of a scientist explaining continental drift on a large projecter. But, once again, *Tidal Wave* has skipped over several scenes—Tetsuro Tamba's second scene in a row as a matter of fact. In *Submersion of Japan* the scene following the eruption is of **a meeting of the Prime Minister's Cabinet detailing how extensive the damage from the eruption and ensuing tsunami were. Following this is a scene of Yamamoto meeting with Dr. Tadokoro and others regarding the earthquake. A scientist eventually stands before a projected image to explain how the earth and its mantle is similar to the shell of an egg. Then he uses a projected film to illustrate how the earth's mantle works. Later, the scientist describes an underwater mountain range** and this eventually leads into the explanation of continental drift, which is where we pick up in *Tidal Wave* (however, **a few reaction shots of the Cabinet** during this scene are excised). In New World's defense, they probably didn't want to dub all of the scientific exposition, which is harder to rewrite than normal dialogue into English.

After the presentation, Tetsuro Tamba finally gets his introduction in *Tidal Wave* in a close-up where he says, in a voice that makes him sound like a brutish imbecile, "The earth moves. It's alive." Preceding this in *Submersion of Japan* there was actually **a shot of Yamamoto contemplating the information. This was followed by a wipe transition**. After this, Yamamoto made the same comment (more or less) in *Submersion of Japan* about the earth moving. Back to *Tidal Wave*, **Tadokoro's warning to the cabinet is shortened and dumbed down** for the U.S. version. It also lacks the ending of the scene, where **Tadokoro abruptly tells the men he has other matters to attend to. After he leaves, the Cabinet discusses Tadokoro, who carries some notoriety despite also having many admirers abroad. Tadokoro then reenters the room because he forgot his glasses. Yamamoto watches him, seeming to be contemplating the man's behavior, as he leaves.** *Tidal Wave* ends with Tadokoro warning the men to prepare for a major catastrophe. There is one reaction shot of Yamamoto and his men, and the scene cuts to what is also the next scene in the Japanese version: Tadokoro's meeting with Prince Watari (Shogo Shimada).

While the two men's conversation about the strange, recent migratory pattern of Swallows (or lack thereof) is intact in *Tidal Wave*, it cuts off the end of the scene. In *Tidal Wave* the scene ends with Watari saying, "I understand," and we cut to a huge explosion at sea. In *Submersion of Japan*, **Tadokoro explains to Watari that as a scientist intuition—or "gut feeling"—is very important to his work. Tadokoro then tears a newspaper in half and uses it to illustrate the theory of continental drift, and also mentions how the man who discovered the fact was laughed at back in 1912 until proven correct after his death. Not long after this we cut to a scene of Tadokoro meeting with several government men (thanks to Watari's influence) including Cabinet Survey Kunie (Tadao Nakamaru); Nakata (Hideaki Nitani), a major in Cognitive Science; and Mimura (Kazuo Kato), Secretary to the Prime Minister. The three men acquire for Tadokoro a submarine, the *Kermadec*, and Tadokoro makes it clear he only wants Onodera as pilot. The scene ends with an earth tremor**, and we cut to an eruption at sea, the scene where we left off in the U.S. version. Although both versions have the same score, in *Tidal Wave* **a radio report explaining an eruption in the Okinawan islands plays,** while in *Submersion of Japan* the radio report plays over the end of the scene between Tadokoro and the three

45

NEW WORLD PICTURES presents
TIDALWAVE

TO 1F—A SUSPENSION BRIDGE IS TOSSED INTO CHURNING WATERS.

NSS 75/121

bureaucrats as they experience the tremor.

Tidal Wave also cuts from the eruption at sea to a shot of Onoda walking through the port. Not so in *Submersion of Japan*, which cuts to **Yoshimura venting angrily to another employee that Onodera has abruptly quit.** This is in keeping with the subplot in the Japanese version that the government is trying to keep Japan's sinking a secret, something *Tidal Wave* doesn't do. Yoshimura has no idea of the destruction awaiting Japan, and simply thinks Onodera has jumped ship to work for another company.

From here, we cut to **Onodera in a cab on his way back home where he receives a message from Reiko informing him that her father died in the recent Izu earthquake. She says that even though "there's no special reason" she really wants to see him again, as she may go travelling abroad.** From here we cut to the shot of Onodera walking through the port as in the U.S. version. However, due to the cut scenes, in the U.S. version we don't even know that the *Wadatsumi* has been replaced by the *Kermadec* (only eagle eyed viewers who took the time to read the sub's names would know). Both versions feature an uncut musical montage of Onodera's voyage on the ship, but *Tidal Wave* cuts to an aerial view of Tokyo once the sequence ends, while *Submersion of Japan* cuts to a scene set within a command center. There, **Tadokoro, Kunie, Nakata, and Mimura inspect a map of the Japan Trench. Then we cut to an exterior view of the ship at dusk, then to Onodera securing the *Kermadec* in a rain storm. We cut to the next day as devices are lowered into the ocean by the crew. Soon it is dusk again, letting us know that some time has elapsed. We cut to Kunie and Nakata discussing the fact that Watari sold some very expensive art to pay for the *Kermadec*. A discussion on his mysterious past and role as a "fixer" in Japanese politics follows. The two stand to look at the map and mention how the Kermadec needs repairs due to being over worked. Mimura walks in and the men discuss how they will leave soon via helicopter to go to Tokyo for a meeting and then fly to the ship to meet with Tadokoro.

We then cut to the aerial shot of Tokyo also present in *Tidal Wave*. However, **the U.S. version dubs in dialogue to explain the men's purpose in Tokyo for the meeting while they are out-of-shot, while the Japanese version of the scene has no dialogue** at all except for when we actually see the three men remarking on the beauty of Tokyo. Both versions cut to a seaplane carrying the three men beginning to land near the ship, but *Tidal Wave* **cuts the landing short**. *Submersion of Japan* shows **the plane land and has several additional scenes set inside the ship with an exhausted looking Onodera reuniting with a coworker, plus a scene of one** of the men fetching Tadokoro in his cabin. We cut to the men inside the ship's meeting room. A very disturbed and disheveled looking Tadokoro soon comes walking into the room and announces he will share his information.

Tidal Wave cuts from the seaplane in midflight to the shot of the disturbed Tadokoro getting ready to address the men. As usual, *Tidal Wave* keeps the first half of the scene where "Tanaka"/Tadokoro explains the earth's shifting mantle, but chops off the latter half to cut straight to a shot of "Tanaka" and the men above deck. In the latter half of the scene deleted from *Tidal Wave*, **Tadokoro's explanation as to what is happening in the Japan Trench is longer and more in depth. Towards the end of his talk he stands and then nearly faints. From here we cut to Tadokoro staggering along the ship's deck. Tadokoro somberly announces that "even a child can figure out what will happen next"—or,

THE LOST FILMS FANZINE PRESENTS MOVIE MILESTONES #3

in other words, Japan will sink. One of the men asks Tadokoro how bad it will be and he explains in greater detail—and this is where *Tidal Wave* picks up.

Unfortunately, actor Kenji Kobayashi's great performance is greatly hindered by the U.S. dub job as he explains the fate that awaits Japan, and in accordance with the U.S. version's title, **"Tanaka" makes sure to mention that there will be great tidal waves,** something he doesn't mention in *Submersion of Japan*. From "Tanaka's" reveal that Japan will sink in *Tidal Wave* we cut straight to the great Tokyo earthquake scene. In *Submersion of Japan*, before the earthquake sequence, Tadokoro makes his prediction and **Masaru Sato's music starts up as the ship violently lurches. We then hear a radio report that the Kanto region was rocked by a massive earthquake.**

The earthquake scene in *Tidal Wave* appears to be uncut, gore and all (glass shards cause some notable blood spatter). *Submersion of Japan* features a scene where an old man who survived the Kanto earthquake of 1923 fears being consumed by fire and is ironically engulfed by a wall of water. **Tidal Wave retains the scene visually but does not dub in this dialogue, and has only grunts and screams** even though it is clear the old man is talking. (If New World didn't want to dub in the dialogue they should have shortened the scene, and considering it has no score it wouldn't have been hard to do.)

Otherwise, the earthquake sequence plays out the same in both versions in terms of footage. Differences reoccur upon the scene's end fade out. In the shot, Yamamoto looks out a window at the fires but **Japanese slates displaying the number of the dead** have been removed from *Tidal Wave*. *Submersion of Japan's* following scene concerns **a memorial for Yamamoto's wife. As Yamamoto burns incense, a narrator informs us that three months have passed since the disaster and law and order is slowly returning to Japan. Yamamoto laments that he was about to quietly finish his term as Prime Minister, but there is no time for the next Cabinet to make plans, so he and his Cabinet must do it. We then cut to Onodera wandering through the wreckage of Tokyo in a brief scene with no dialogue. We then cut to the D1 HQ where Kunie and another official wonder if an earthquake even worse than the previous one is coming. Soon Onodera walks in and is informed that Tadokoro is meeting with the Prime Minister to discuss the D2 plan. Kunie explains that they have come to the end of D1 (investigating the cause of the sinking) and that D2 (an evacuation plan) commences next. Kunie also informs Onodera that they will charter *Wadatsumi I* and *II* to continue monitoring the situation. Outside, as Onodera enters a vehicle, he is attacked by his former *Wadatsumi* co-pilot Yuki (Isao Natsuyagi) for not telling him why he left the company. Yuki's anger is based out of affection for his friend however, not malice, and he soon reveals that he wishes to be his co-pilot. During their conversation he also reveals that Reiko has been calling to look for him. And from there we cut to a woodland panning shot set to Saito's poignant score.

The tail end of this panning shot is present in *Tidal Wave* with the **score removed**. To backtrack in terms of *Tidal Waves*' editing, this shot very sloppily follows the fadeout from the scene of Yamamoto watching Tokyo burn. The important bits of the meeting with Watari are retained, but **a shot of Onodera gazing at Watari's maid servant, Hanae (Yuriko Horn), and imagining Reiko** is removed. Also, preceding an earth tremor, **shots of birds flying away and a close up of Tadokoro** are cut. The scene ends in both versions with discussion of the D2 evacuation plan, but *Tidal Wave* cuts to a map of Australia when the scene ends. *Submersion of Japan* continues with **a budget meeting between the Prime Minister and two advisors**. Some heated discussion follows about government

THE LOST FILMS FANZINE PRESENTS MOVIE MILESTONES #3

reform and the evacuation (specifically, what if it turns out Japan isn't really sinking?). Following this is the map shot of Australia as in the U.S. cut. In *Tidal Wave*, **Japanese text identifying Canberra and the Prime Minister's country villa** are removed though the shots are the same otherwise. Naturally, **Japanese subtitles** are removed from the scene in which both the Australian Prime Minister (Andrew Hughes) and the Japanese representative speak English.

The way the scene is handled in *Tidal Wave* is debatable. Throughout *Tidal Wave's* English dub, the Japanese actors speak normally and are not given Asian accents. In this scene, however, the Japanese representative Nozaki (Nobuo Nakamura) is given an accent and speaks slowly in slightly broken English just as he does in the original version (though the voice is different). Both versions end with Nozaki giving the Australian Prime Minister a precious Buddha stat-

ue. Following this is a scene between the Australian Prime Minister and his aid where the former states that he'd rather accept more art treasures than people and he worries the Japanese will build a new country on his soil. Furthermore, *Tidal Wave* scores the scene with Sato's music, while in the Japanese version it is **unscored.** From his remark that he'd rather accept art treasures than people in *Tidal Wave*, and after the full scene in *Submersion of Japan*, we cut to a series of images representing world capitals ending with New York.

Finally in *Tidal Wave*, after 45 minutes (over halfway into the 80 minute movie), we get to the Lorne Greene footage. In the new scene, **a Japanese representative, Narita (John Fujioka), is appealing to Ambassador Warren Richards (Greene), whom he has known for many years, to help negotiate and encourage other nations to help take in the Japanese before it is too late. Through Narita, the tid-**

al wave aspect is again emphasized and a new plot line is introduced. Narita tells Richards that, "The tidal waves that threaten to destroy Japan are the results of changes in the earth's crust at the floor of the pacific ocean. These changes could affect your own pacific coast as well." Richards then mentions how astrologers have been predicting that California would plunge into the ocean for many years as well—his point being that he needs more proof of Japan's imminent demise before he can take action. With that the scene ends and we cut back to the Japanese footage where Prime Minister Yamamoto is being briefed once again.

To return to *Submersion of Japan*, after the international montage of world capital shots, we cut to a scene of Onodera at the D2 HQ receiving word that his mother has died. Soon another man walks into the room revealing that Tadokoro has gone public with the news prematurely and will soon be on television. Following this revelation is Dr. Tadokoro's interview on live TV. The men in the control room then watch the impassioned interview, and we cut back and forth between the men in the control room and Tadokoro in the studio. When a reporter makes light of Tadokoro's claims, Tadokoro strikes the man. Tadokoro must be restrained, and as he looks madly into the camera we cut to a distressed Watari watching from home. Hanae shuts the television off and opens his sliding doors so that he may look outside.

The next scene has Nakata being attacked by Yukinaga (Yusuke Takita) while Kunie and Onodera restrain him. The reason Yukinaga attacks Nakata is that he was the one who set up the interview knowing full well Tadokoro was not the best messenger to break the news to the public, which actually still had not been OK'd by the Japanese government. At the moment, Tadokoro is being labeled as a quack and it is the end of his career more or less. Nakata argues that it is better for the government to acknowledge the truth rather than have it leak out through a foreign nation seeing as how D2 negotiations are in progress. Onodera states that he feels sorry for Tadokoro having been the one to discover their impending doom.

The next scene concerns the Prime Minister meeting with Watari who hands him the official plan for D2. Watari lays out three options. One is for the Japanese to establish a new home country somehow, the other is for them to integrate into other countries, and the last one suggests they die together as a people and take no action. From a shot of Yamamoto with tears in his eyes we cut to an Osaka Expressway, and then to the inside of a car transporting Onodera and his older brother (Nitta Masao). The two go to a restaurant to have a drink and Onodera's brother informs him he has received a job offer in Canada. Onodera encourages him strongly to go, but he can't actually tell him that Japan is sinking, so his brother is suspicious of Onodera's insistence that he take the job as soon as possible. Onodera imagines himself telling his brother to leave the country because it will soon sink, but restrains himself from actually doing so. (Remember, Japanese citizens do not yet believe Tadokoro's claims and simply thinks he's a quack, and Onodera still feels obliged to keep his silence for the government.) We then cut to Onodera drunkenly walking through a huge crowd in nighttime Osaka. This scene is present in the U.S. cut, but it has been reshuffled and trimmed slightly (more on that later).

Back to *Tidal Wave*—where we left off with the new Lorne Greene footage—

51

THE LOST FILMS FANZINE PRESENTS MOVIE MILESTONES #3

we cut to a government briefing scene from *Submersion of Japan* that doesn't occur until after Onodera's streetwalking scene in Osaka which we have yet to see in *Tidal Wave*. As such, this is the first instance of *Tidal Wave* rearranging footage. The briefing explains just how Japan will sink and when—within ten short months. "Only ten," Yamamoto mutters, shocked, and we cut to a drunken Onodera walking through the crowds skipping over the scenes with his brother as that subplot was excised from *Tidal Wave*. As he wanders through the crowd **Onodera thinks aloud of Reiko** but in the Japanese version we have no insight into his inner thoughts. And, once again the dub job here really makes the U.S. version suffer. In the Japanese version, as Onodera walks through the crowd, **images of his brother running from the future destruction play out in Onodera's mind** (the images being superimposed over shots of the crowd). **Onodera also tells all the people he sees to run away in his head.** Eventually, in both versions, Onodera runs into Reiko in the street by chance.

Tidal Wave has an **iris wipe transition** that cuts to the couple in bed together. *Submersion of Japan* cuts from Reiko's smiling face to the government briefing scene partially shown in *Tidal Wave* before Onodera's walk through Osaka. *Submersion of Japan* features an introduction to the scene not present in *Tidal Wave* where there is an introduction to the talk and **a countdown of sorts to the simulation** (*Tidal Wave* begins the scene right when the simulation starts). The scene is shortened overall in *Tidal Wave*, which cuts back a **great deal of scientific explanation.** This is followed by **a meeting scene in the Diet among the cabinet discussing when and how the Japanese people should be told the country will sink in 10 months.** Following this is a scene of Prime Minister Yamamoto addressing the financial and industrial leaders in private about the crisis and how they are to help evacuate Japan, such as improving and constructing new airplane runways and converting tanker ships into transport ships for citizens. This is followed by a scene of Onodera and Nakata discussing the fact that Onodera's job is now over. Onodera reveals he plans to marry Reiko and leave the country ASAP. He then asks about Tadokoro, and Nakata answers he doesn't know where he is.

After this we cut to the scene of Onodera and Reiko in bed, the scene where we last left off discussing in *Tidal Wave*. Some of the scene's early moments without dialogue are cut from *Tidal Wave*. In *Tidal Wave* **Reiko tells "Onoda" of how she searched everywhere for him**, but she says nothing of this in *Submersion of Japan*, where **she explains how much she loves scuba diving and the isolation she feels,** which mirrors Onodera's feelings when he is deep underwater. In *Tidal Wave* the greatly abbreviated scene ends when **Reiko tells "Onoda" she never wants to lose him again.** We then cut to images of newspapers announcing the tragedy (the shots are the same as from *Submersion of Japan* only **Japanese subtitles** translating the papers have naturally been eliminated). In *Submersion of Japan*, the bed scene has a **wipe fade** to sometime later when the two are dressed and preparing to leave. Onodera orders to Reiko to buy tickets to Geneva as soon as possible as he has clearly divulged to her the classified information. In a scene more relevant to Japanese culture than Western sensibilities, **Onodera tells Reiko that he's still not sure whether or not he's in love with her, but if he could make it with anyone it would probably be her.** (It's no surprise that this scene was cut for Westerners who would no doubt find it odd.)

From here in *Submersion of Japan* we cut to **Onodera walking down the street in a brief shot, and then to Watari, Hanae, and Kunie riding in a car together. Kunie informs Watari that Mt. Fuji is becoming more and more unstable. Watari tells Hanae how beautiful Fuji looks today and they take a longing glance at the mountain. The next scene has the Geodesic Society of America in a meeting discussing Japan's impending doom, thus officially letting the cat out of the bag to the world—including the Japanese public.**

Following this scene in *Submersion of Japan* is the newspapers seen in *Tidal Wave*. Then Yamamoto holds his press conference to announce the news to the world, but **the U.S. version has Yamamoto specifically mention Japan being destroyed by tidal waves**, which he doesn't mention in the original. Once this scene ends, in *Tidal Wave*, we cut to "Onoda" and Reiko in the hotel room getting dressed as the scene has been reshuffled. In *Tidal Wave's* version of the hotel scene, **Reiko mentions going to say goodbye to her father at Mt. Fuji before she leaves.** Onoda's comment about not knowing whether or not he's in love is redubbed to be a conversation about **whether or not they are both selfish for leaving their loved ones behind.** We then cut to a shot of Onodera walking down the street, and then to him sitting in headquarters feeling optimistic, about to leave the country (this scene follows Yamamoto's press conference scene in *Submersion of Japan*). The scene is truncated in *Tidal Wave* and is missing a few bits of dialogue, notably **Onodera giving Nakata and Mimura his address in Switzerland. He also asks them to look out for Yuki while he's away.**

After the eruption of Mt. Fuji, both versions cut to New York. This is the first case where the two versions intersect à la *Godzilla, King of the Monsters!* and the new U.S. star is edited into the original Japanese footage. *Submersion of Japan* features a U.N. discussion about the current situation in Japan and in *Tidal Wave* Lorne Greene has been edited into this same sequence. However, aside from the occasional **close-up of Greene**, the footage is all from *Submersion of Japan*. Essentially the two scenes are the same except for *Tidal Wave* cuts out **a representative from the Middle East who speaks of the difficulty of dealing with refugees from Palestine and speculates that there will be** similar problems with the displaced Japanese.

From here both versions cut to a shot of Tokyo Bay (only minus the **Japanese slates** in *Tidal Wave*). Both versions feature Yamamoto watching evacuation efforts via television. *Tidal Wave* then cuts back to the U.N. where **Richards addresses the delegates making an impassioned plea for nations to open up their borders to the Japanese.** This cuts to an aerial view of Japan in chaos. Back to the Japanese version, following Yamamoto's scene watching the evacuation, we cut to **a D2 control room where Nakata and his comrades express their concern about not being able to evacuate Japan quickly enough. Next is a brief meeting scene between Yamamoto and some of his Cabinet.** Following this is a scene between Yamamoto and Watari regarding the extinction of the dinosaurs and the earth's changing climate. Yamamoto then tells Watari he shall travel overseas to beg for his peoples' lives directly. Yamamoto says that if they refuse to take ten million he will beg for one million and so on until the number dwindles to only 100. Their talk is interrupted by a call from Nakata informing them that the submersion is happening sooner than anticipated. From there we cut to the aerial view of Japan seen in *Tidal Wave* only said film cuts out an **additional aerial shot of the Kii Peninsula.**

The next altered scene involves two cameramen flying over Osaka, which is **trimmed slightly** in *Tidal Wave*. After this scene ends we cut to another high altitude view of Japan as it sinks, but in *Submersion of Japan* we cut to **a scene of Kunie and Watari discussing D2.** This is followed by the destruction of the Sanriku Coast. In *Tidal Wave*, first we get the high altitude view of Japan, and then the destruction of Sanriku. After this in *Submersion of Japan* is the aerial shot of the Tohoku District which appears before this in *Tidal Wave*. Also, there are **additional shots of Hokkaido from space, and then an aerial view of the Kinki District** in *Submersion of Japan*. Then we cut to a shot of people boarding boats bound for Korea in both versions. In both cuts Reiko can be seen watching the boats on the cliff, but ***Tidal Wave* gives Reiko an inner monologue making it appear as though she plans to board the boats and go to Korea.**

From the ensuing tsunami scene where the people on said boats are killed, both versions cut to high altitude shots of Japan, the only differences are that **Richard's voice can be heard talking about the crisis** in *Tidal Wave* while *Submersion of Japan* is silent and includes **slates identifying Okinawa and the other islands of Japan** as they sink. We then cut to **Richards explaining that 34 million lives have been saved so far but there is still work to be done and more lives to be saved.** The Japanese version too cuts to a U.N. scene, minus Richards of course. The *Tidal Wave* version of the scene more or less follow's the Japanese version's continuity only **here it is Richards that hands the floor over to Eugene Cox (Van Henry) of the U.S. Geological Society** who explains that when Japan breaks in two at the 'central zone' the rescue efforts should be recalled because it will be too late. (To be clear, the Cox character is from the original *Submersion of Japan* footage, it's just made to look like Richards gives him the floor.) We then cut back to the Japanese footage within a command center which observes that the central zone is indeed moving.

Both versions feature a montage of images of Onodera in a magazine working to save as many Japanese as he can as he searches for Reiko. In *Tidal Wave*, **Richards is shown to be reading the magazine and talks to his secretary**

THE LOST FILMS FANZINE PRESENTS MOVIE MILESTONES #3

This Super 8mm version of SUBMERSION OF JAPAN oddly has the Gilman on it along with a UFO!

Fran (Rhonda Leigh Hopkins) about what a remarkable young man he is. When Fran asks him how much longer the rescue operation will last, Richards answers not long because soon Japan will sink and there will be no one left to rescue. We then cut to a shot of Watari's wheelchair covered in ash as Richards finishes his dialogue which leads into the farewell scene between Yamato, Watari, and Tadokoro.

Before we discuss the penultimate scene, in *Submersion of Japan*, **the conversation about Onodera's heroics and the continuing sinking of Japan is had by the Australian Prime Minister** instead of Richards. From here we cut to **Kunie, Nakata and Mimura receiving word from Yamamoto over an intercom that D Plan has come to an end as time has run out. The three men silently react to the news, switch off their equipment, and one steps outside into the sunlight revealing they are on a ship at sea. Nakata and Mimura go out on deck where Nakata collapses from exhaustion. Mimura looks over the railing and wonders aloud what happened to Onodera and Tadokoro.** We then cut to Watari's ash covered wheelchair.

The farewell between Hanae, Watari and Yamamoto is mostly intact but cuts out some **dramatic pauses** here and there to speed up the action. Naturally, the exchange between Yamamoto and "Tanaka" is shortened greatly in *Tidal Wave* and "Tanaka" does not deliver the touching eulogy for Japan that Tadokoro does. In *Submersion of Japan*, **Tadokoro compares the Japanese people to infants losing their mother in the form of Japan's destruction.** In both cuts, Tadokoro stays behind to die with Watari and Japan, while Yamamoto and Hanae board a helicopter to leave Japan forever.

The final moments of *Tidal Wave*—in which Reiko and Onodera/Onoda are revealed to be alive, but on different trains on opposite sides of the world—is the same as in *Submersion of Japan* with only minor differences in sound and titles. As the camera pans back from the sinking Japan in *Tidal Wave*, a **rushing wind** can be heard, while in the original it is **silent**. When a train carrying Reiko comes into frame in the snow, **Japanese slates appear reading "Somewhere on earth"** but *Tidal Wave* has no slates of any kind. In both versions we cut to a train coursing through a desert terrain with Onodera/"Onoda" on board. As he looks outside **"The End"** replaces **"Owari"** in *Tidal Wave*.

JAPAN SINKS ON TV

The cast and crew of SUBMERSION OF JAPAN's TV series. From right to left: Keiju Kobayashi, Toshio Kurosawa, Kaoru Yumi, Mari Christine, Takenori Murano, Mari Tomoe, Nakamura Kojiro, and Toshiyuki Hosokawa.

Though many westerners saw *Submersion of Japan* through its U.S. release as *Tidal Wave* in 1975, most have never seen, and are unaware of the accompanying TV series. And how did this series come about? Supposedly, there was a stipulation in Sakyo Komatsu's contract with Toho that a TV series based on the movie be aired on Tokyo Broadcasting System after the film came out. As such, the TV version was shot simultaneously (to an extent) with the film.

What would typically occur is that on days for SPFX footage the TV crew might film the same footage with TV cameras. (The series' Japanese wiki page claims that a few bits filmed by the TV crew made it into the movie, though this sounds a little confusing.)

It should also be noted that the series wasn't a sequel but a TV version of the concept and different actors portray all the roles except for Keiju Kobayashi as Dr. Tadokoro (to differentiate the character's appearance, this version sports a mustache). Takenori Murano played Onodera and as Reiko was Kaoru Yumi, a popular Japanese starlet who appeared in *Prophecies of Nostradamus* in 1974 for Toho. (Sakyo Komatsu wanted her cast in the movie as Reiko, so perhaps her role on the series was something of a consolation prize?)

The series was produced by Toho's top talent, including Tomoyuki Tanaka, and Jun Fukuda, who even directed the first episode "Scattering Sea." Future Godzilla series SPFX director Koichi Kawakita was also among the special effects staff but not the main director.

Each episode of the series more or less focused on seeing a new location or Japanese city sink beneath the waves and was preceded with an announcement that what the viewer was seeing was not newsreel footage, but a dramatiza-

SMALL SCREEN SUBMERSION

tion. Famous landmarks destroyed in the series included Kamakura's famous Buddha statue, the temples and castles of Kyoto, and Osaka Castle, which literally floats away during one episode's end. Komatsu even joked about the format of the series telling *Science Fiction Studies* that, "The novel described this gradual submergence of Japan by focusing on a few different areas, but in the television series, different locales would go under every week. As if they were telling people, 'Stay tuned for the destruction of YOUR city!' (Laughs)."

The series premiered on October 6, 1974 to fairly healthy ratings that had dwindled by the time the finale aired on March 30, 1975. It was a 55-minute program that aired Sunday nights at 8:00 PM. Hiroshi Itsuki sang the theme song "Tomorrow's Love." The series also contained guest appearances by well-known Toho actors like Katsuhiko Sasaki (*Godzilla vs. Megalon*), Yoshio Tsuchiya (*The Human Vapor*), Yu Fujiki (a popular comedy star), Kenji Sahara, Kunie Tanaka, and Mie Hama (*You Only Live Twice*). Shin Kishida (the INTERPOL agent in *Godzilla vs. Mechagodzilla*) did the voiceover narration for the "next episode" teasers.

An outline of the first eight episodes was posted by a Japanese blogger, but the translation leaves a lot to be desired. The gist of the pilot, from what I can gather, is that Onodera's fiancé (not Reiko) dies in an earthquake. Onodera blames Tadokoro for not predicting it, which gets their relationship off to a rocky start.

The second episode had Onodera and Tadokoro arguing about how deep to dive, and Onodera suffers some sort of injury that is so serious that it could lead to him losing his right hand! Onodera soon after meets Reiko at her villa at Izu. Nearby Mt. Amagi explodes in front of the duo who run away from an ensuing tidal wave. According to the blogger the scene was not a special ef-

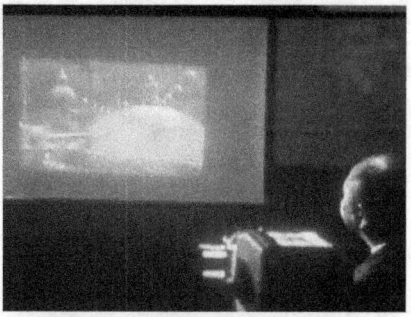

Several screengrabs from the series showing various miniatures and SPFX shots.

The new Reiko and Onodera: Kaoru Yumi and Takenori Murano.

fect and the crew happened to catch a huge wave on film apparently.

The theme of episode three was apparently tension between the older generation and the younger one about how to face Japan's sinking. The beginning destruction of Himeji Castle served as the centerpiece. The destruction of the castle continued into episode four, which also explored Tadokoro's past, specifically how he lost his wife and child. Apparently Dr. Tadokoro had a daughter named Maria, who he is reunited with for the first time in 20 years. Meanwhile, Onodera's romance with Reiko continues.

Episode five was about the sinking of Ogasawara Island. Knowing it will sink, Tadokoro observes it to get a better idea of how Japan would sink. Not all the islanders evacuate on time and a small boy runs back into his schoolhouse to retrieve a picture. The boy dies and a prominent shot had the photo floating atop the sea. Episode six was about ways to possibly save Japan, and episode seven revolved around the draining of Lake Ashi due to Japan's sinking. (I wonder if Toho reused a similar scene from *Godzilla vs. Megalon*?) The episode also brought a plot point from the novel that wasn't in the film. It mentions how Reiko's father is building an underwater amusement park. Also, he doesn't want Onodera and Reiko to marry.

Episode eight was about predicting another Kanto earthquake, though the episode's destruction scenes comprised of a dam breaking and flooding a village. Episode nine, which is the last that the blogger reviews, was about a lost Japanese civilization that sunk into the sea Atlantis style many years ago. Specifically, they used the Kumaso tribe from the Yamato Takeru story for the lost city. Another question raised in the episode is: will the Japanse be persecuted like the Jews when they seek solace in other countries?

What happens in the remaining story arc is hard to piece together up to the final episode. While in the film Onodera and Reiko are separated, in the TV series it is revealed they both escape to Australia. Also, the big Tokyo earthquake that takes place in the middle of the film serves instead as the series finale. The final scene of the series saw Reiko and Onodera bidding farewell to Dr. Tadokoro who, in the film, chose to die with Japan. Not so here, as Dr. Tadokoro is airlifted via chopper, though there's apparently not room for the two lovers. The duo run to the highest point in Japan that has yet to sink. An earth tremor separates them and Reiko falls down a slope. The lovers then spend a long time reaching for one another until they finally grasp hands. (This is very similar to Toei's final scene in 1977's *Legend of Dinosaurs and Monster Birds.*) The series freeze frames on that image, though we can hear a helicopter coming (meaning they are probably about to be resuced). And indeed, a postscript to the series later revealed that they were rescued and went to Australia.

Komatsu himself was not overly impressed with this adaptation, and didn't even bother watching it until many years later. "I didn't get a chance to see the television version when it aired, but I was able to see it for the first time recently on DVD. It wasn't very good."

EPISODE GUIDE
MAIN CREW: Directed by Takashi Nagano, Minoru Kanaya, Jun Fukuda, Kiyoshi Nishimura, Eizo Yamagiwa, and Tadashi Mabune
Written by Yuichiro Yamane, Hideka Nagasaka, and Toshiro Ishido
Produced by Tomoyuki Tanaka, Susumu Saito, Hitoshi Ogura, Yoji Hashimoto, and Takao Yasuda
Music by Kenjiro Hirose
Starring Keiju Kobayashi, Takenori Murano, Kaoru Yumi, Mari Christine, Tomoko Ogawa, Toshiyuki Hosokawa, Toshio Kurosawa

Air Date/ Episode Title/ Writer/ Director/Guest Stars Note: When writer or director are not given, that means they directed the subsequent episode, and writer and/or director are not credited again until a new one takes over.

1. October 6, 1974 "Scattering Sea" Yuichiro Yamane/Jun Fukuda/ Mariko Mochizuki (Etsuko Morishita), Masami Shimojo (Shinsuke Morishita), Munemaru Koda (Professor), Hajime Izu (Professor), Kazuko Imai (Etsuko's mother)

2. October 13, 1974 "Undersea Frenzy" Yuichiro Yamane/Kiyoshi Nishimura/ Mariko Mochizuki (Etsuko Morishita), Katsuhiko Sasaki (Tsuchiya), Hajime

Izu (Professor), Munemaru Koda (Professor), Yoshio Katsube (Technical Official)

3. October 20, 1974 "White Crack" Yuichiro Yamane/ Kiyoshi Nishimura/ Setsuko Sekine (Jun), Tomoe Mari (Kyoko), Katsumi Ishiyama (Friend of Onodera)

4. October 27, 1974 "When the Sea Collapses"/Takashi Nagano/Toshie Shoji

5. November 3, 1974 "The Island is Sinking Now"/Shukei Nagasaka/ Kunio Murai (Shunsuke Kinukawa), Tetsuro Tsuno (Teacher Yajima), Tsunehiro Arai (Taichi), Mika Katsuragi (Nurse), Michio Kida (islander)

6. November 10, 1974 "The Earth Groaning in Sadness"/Kiyoshi Nishimura/Kunio Murai (Shunsuke Kinukawa), Kazuya Oguri (Senzo Onodera), Takao Zushi (Kazuhiko Sasaki), Hiroya Morita (Deputy Director Gomiya)

7. November 17, 1974 "Sky Fangs, Black Dragon Rolls"/ Yuichiro Yamane

8. November 24, 1974 "A Muddy Stream of Anger"/Eizo Yamagiwa/Kan Yanagiya (Gen-san), Tatsuo Matsushita (Professor), Munemaru Koda (Professor), Yoshio Katsube (Technical Officer), Hajime Izu (Professor)

9. December 1, 1974 "The Mystery of the Undersea Cave"/Toshiro Ishido/ Owadabaku (Haruo Tokumitsu), Isao Tamagawa (Tokumitsu FutoshiTasukuEmon), Ken Mitsuda (Yoshio Onishi)

10. December 8, 1974 "Aso Fire Falls"/ Shukei Nagasaka/Minoru Kanaya/ Masaaki Daimon (Kenji Okita), Harumi Arai (Reiko Kitagawa), Toshio Takahara (Reiko's father), Masahiko Kametani (Norihiko Aoki)

11. December 15, 1974 "Aurora in Kyoto!!"/Yuichiro Yamane/ Takahiko Higashino (Hidaka), Tomoe Mari (Kyoko)

12. December 22, 1974 "Dangerous Capital of Kyoto"/Mafune Sada/ Takahiko Tono (Hidaka), Junko Natsu (Tomoko Yoshikawa), Jun Negami (Kozo Kimura)

13. December 29, 1974 "Crumbling Kyoto"/Junko Natsu (Tomoko Yoshikawa), Jun Negami (Kozo Kimura), Tony Cetera (Professor Douglas)

14. January 5, 1975 "Tomorrow's Love"/Shukei Nagasaka/Takashi Nagano/Hiroshi Itsuki (Shogo Katsura), Takanobu Hozumi (Kiyoyoshi Otaguro), Hiroshi Yagyu (Assistant Director)

15. January 12, 1975 "Large Explosion/ Undersea Oil Field"/Mie Hama (Kazumi Yamauchi), Shinichi Yanagisawa (Yasaku Yamauchi), Katsutoshi Atarashi (Seiji Hamakura), Franz Gruber (Robert Custer)

16. January 19, 1975 "Kagoshima Bay SOS!" Yuichiro Yamane/Eizo Yamagiwa/Miyako Tasaka (Yukari Yuki), Takashi Kanda (Ushiyama)

17. January 26, 1975 "Amakusa Has Disappeared!" Kikuo Hayashiya (Kazuo Sakamoto), Sumio Takatsu (Koichi Ariyoshi), Toyoko Takechi (Haru Sakamoto)

18. February 2, 1975 "Ogouchi Dam in Crisis"/Kiyoshi Nishimura/ Atomu Shimojo (Saburo Nagai), Aki Mizusawa (Naoko Nihonmatsu), Yu Fujiki (Yasugoro Nihonmatsu), Tomiko Ishii (Wife of Yasugoro)

19. February 9, 1975 "Farewell, the

Town of Hakodate"/Shukei Nagasaka/ Minoru Kanaya/ Noriko Sengoku (Hana Hojo), Pepe Hozumi (Motota Inoue), Midori Takei (Yuri Hojo), Hideaki Obara (Goro), Kazuhiro Fukuzaki (Kazuo), Takaki Nabeya (Shigeru)

20. February 16, 1975 "Sinking Hokkaido"/Sakura Kamo (Iku Hattori), Kojiro Kusanagi (Kumayoshi Wada), Kazunori Emura (Sasuke), Keiji Sakakida (Father of Iku)

21. February 23, 1975 "Izu Oshima Scattered on the Pillar of Fire" Takashi Nagano/Yoshio Yoshida (Kemon Shimamoto), Michiyo Yamazoe (Taeko Shimamoto), Toyoto Fukuda (Kenichiro Osaki)

22. March 2, 1975 "The Japanese Archipelago That Bends"/Yuichiro Yamane/ Ichiro Ogura (Junichi Ishiguro), Noriko Kitazawa (Fusayo Ishiguro), Yoshio Tsuchiya (Yoshio Tsuchiya), Hiroyuki Takano (Koji Ishiguro), Ako Nakamura (Sachiko Ishiguro), Kunihisa Mizutani (Cape Oura Lighthouse, Kosato), Kazuo Suzuki (Cape Oura Lighthouse Kitchener, Kishimoto)

23. March 9, 1975 "Kamakura Disappeared into the Sea"/Minoru Kanaya/ Kenji Todoroki (Nisa Oki), Yasufumi Torozawa (Self-Defense Forces member)

24. March 16, 1975 "Tokyo Citizens, Escape"/Kenji Todoroki (Nisa Oki), Yasufumi Torozawa (Self-Defense Forces member), Paula Nozawa (Emmy)

25. March 23, 1975 "Tokyo Sinks"/Jun Fukuda   /Kenji Todoroki (Nisa Oki), Yasufumi Morizawa (Self-Defense Forces member), Hatsuko Wakahara (Okayama)

26. March 30, 1975 "Last Day in Tokyo Ban"/ Kojika (Ginji Matsumoto), Machiko Soga (Teruko Matsumoto)

Keiji Kobayashi returned to portary Tadokoro, seen here with Reiko and Onodera.

COMPANION PIECE:

© 1974/1975 TSUBURAYA PRODUCTIONS

During the 1974-1975 TV season, on Sunday nights viewers could choose to turn into not one, but two Sakyo Komatsu related projects back to back. Because, before *Submersion of Japan* began its broadcast for the evening, viewers could tune into another series Komatsu was working on: *The Monkey Army*. Better known in the U.S. as a direct-to-video compilation movie called *Time of the Apes*, the series was a Japanese take on *Planet of the Apes*.

In fact, the series was conceived of shortly after a TV broadcast of the 1968 original *Planet of the Apes* scored huge ratings. At the same time, monsters like Godzilla were losing popularity in theaters, and the Ultraman franchise was likewise beginning to lag on TV.

Ultraman's producer, Tsuburaya Productions, took note of the popularity of both of Panic Movies and the old *Apes* films and decided to do a TV series based on that idea. To do so they asked Komatsu to be one of their writers and he obliged. Along with Komatsu to plot the series was Aritsune Toyota and Koji Tanaka.

Komatsu and the planning staff held meetings for the series twice a month at a hotel in Akasaka. A lawyer for TBS analyzed the story and concluded that it was different enough from the 20th Century Fox property that they could proceed.

Though it was thought of as a kid's series to a degree, Komatsu took his research very seriously in terms of the apes. For instance, in real life chimpanzees are much more aggressive than go-

THE MONKEY ARMY

This still offers a good look at the primary cast (where humans are concerned at least). From left to right are Masaaki Kaji (Jiro), Hiroko Saito (Yurika), Reiko Tokunaga (Kazuko) and Tetsuya Ushio (Godo). © 1974/1975 TSUBURAYA PRODUCTIONS

rillas. In the *Apes* movies, gorillas were aggressive and chimps were pacifists. Komatsu switched this in the name of accuracy, with chimps now serving as aggressors. Komatsu also brought in baboons into the mix, while the *Apes* series never did. Another way in which the series differentiated itself from the movies was that the apes' society looked similar to modern day rural Japan, which was, of course, just a budgetary necessity. Nor could the series afford elaborate makeup, and so all the actors wore ape masks (50 were constructed in all at a cost of 50,000 yen).

The protagonists consisted of a young woman, a young man, and two children. The main protagnoist was Kazuko Izumi, a 22-year-old scientist at a cryogenics lab, led by Dr. Sasaki (a minor character who only appears in the first and last episodes). One day Sasaki's nephew Jiro (12) comes to visit with his friend Yurika (15). When an earthquake hits, Kazuko, Yurika, and Jiro take refuge in some cryogenic capsules. They awaken over a thousand years later in a world ruled by hostile apes. The trio escapes the apes and band together with another human, Godo, and a young female ape sympathetic to their plight named Pepe. The friends go on the run from the apes until they discover a mysterious UFO, which is the emissary of an all-powerful computer.

This is where the story becomes in-

THE LOST FILMS FANZINE PRESENTS MOVIE MILESTONES #3

teresting. To its credit, this plotline precedes the Skynet concept from the Terminator films. In this case, the Skynet precursor is called Universal Ecosystem Control Computer (UECCOM). Mankind created it at a time when their population suddenly and alarmingly began to decrease. To make up for the lack of humans, apes were trained as labor workers similar to *Conquest of the Planet of the Apes*. Eventually the apes rebelled, and UECOM sided with them.

When our heroes confront the organization's super computer, it demands they be sent to another planet or to the future to end conflict between the apes. While Godo refuses and is sent to another planet, Kazuko, Yurika and Jiro mysteriously awaken not in the future but in the past which they have just left.

Unfortunately, this series struggled in the ratigs against more popular series, like the mega-hit *Space Battleship Yamato* which aired in the same time slot. As such, it received no sequel series from Tsuburaya. It has no official release in the U.S. outside of an OOP VHS of *Time of the Apes* (released through Sandy Frank in 1987). However, with Mill Creek licensing many Tsuburaya properties, we can hope that perhaps there's a chance it could be released.

THE LOST FILMS FANZINE PRESENTS MOVIE MILESTONES #3

Above: Screengrab of the main characters meeting Godo for the first time. Take note of Pepe (Kazue Takita), the heroes' ape friend who is based upon a a Lar Gibbon (originally, the character was envisioned as an orangutan). Page opposite: Godo in trouble with the Monkey Army as usual. © 1974/1975 TSUBURAYA PRODUCTIONS

If you've only seen THE MONKEY ARMY via TIME OF THE APES (VHS backcover to the left), then you didn't get to see the character of Tip, the friendly robot who aids the heroes (but was killed off before the final episode).

65

AFTER JAPAN SINKS!!!

Plans for a sequel to 1973's biggest hit movie (actually, the most successful Japanese film of the 1970s), began right away in 1974. In early spring, a small speed poster appeared in Toho theaters advertising *Continuation: Sinking of Japan* stating, "Are the Japanese who lost their homeland obliterated from world history?" Likewise, *Famous Monsters of Filmland* in America also reported on *After Japan Sinks*. Toho had initially hoped this to be their big 1975 summer release, but Sakyo Komatsu had no concrete ideas at this time, and Toho wanted his vision.

Then came another trade ad for the film in 1976 by Toho. This time the catchphrase read, "30 million Japanese who lost their homeland! Ethnic energy that explodes in persecution, to Europe, to the United States, to Australia!" The Toho lineup for 1978 again announced the film touting, "30 million Japanese people scattered from the sinking archipelago to the world! In persecution conflict, they were organized and a nation without a land was born!" This would almost seem to imply the Japanese try to gain another landmass to call home. In any case, this was sadly the last anyone heard of a sequel to Toho's 1973 *Submersion of Japan*. In the late 1970s, Toho had been embroiled in an ill-fated co-production with Hammer called *Nessie*, which killed/delayed a number of other Toho films. This, in addition to the 1978 Godzilla Revival meeting, likely led to the abandonment of the *Submersion of Japan* sequel.

And how does one follow up a movie called *Submersion of Japan* with a sequel when at the end of the first film, Japan had mostly sank? As one can see from the taglines in the previous paragraph, the film would have focused more so on the survival of the Japanese people over more natural disasters. However, the ending of the first film doesn't actually show the entire continent disappear into the ocean, and perhaps the sequel would have begun with that very scene? As for other details, the film's Japanese wikipedia page states that it would concern Onodera and Reiko finally finding one another in Switzerland.

While the details of the aborted film sequel are scarce (it's possible no treatment of any kind was ever written), Sakyo Komatsu finally wrote a sequel to his novel in 2006. At the time 75 years old, Komatsu teamed with younger writer Tani Koshu to pen it. Titled *Japan Sinks, Part II* and published by Shogakukan, Komatsu envisioned the sequel focusing on the effects that the sinking of Japan had on the rest of the world. In this new story, volcanic ash from the eruptions would have plunged the world into a colder climate which causes a food shortage. In an interview, Komatsu specifically mentioned these two ideas being "global cooling" and "the end of the Japanese people".

In the finished book, the story picks up 25 years after Japan has sunk. With forty million Japanese dead from the sinking, the population now sits at 80 million people scattered across the world. The Japanese have settled in places as diverse as Papua New Guinea, Kazakhstan, and even the Amazon River in South America. In some cases, the Japanese live better than the locals due to their different lifestyle, while in other areas they are shunned and persecuted.

The remaining Japanese government has created a new plan to reunify their people. It is called the Megafloat—huge artificial islands that can hold 1 million people each are to be set in the ocean where Japan once stood. Developed alongside this is the "Earth Simulator" which can predict the future of the environment and the future looks grim. According to the simulator, a new ice age will soon devastate agriculture in the Northern Hemisphere. The simulator predicts that a billion people will die in the next thirty years. When Japan warns the world, the U.S. and China try to manipulate Japan's Megafloat project to their own ends. A conflict then emerges between the Prime Minister, who feels the Japanese should keep the technology to themselves, and the Foreign Minister, who feels Japan should use this as a way to further integrate with the rest of the world. The book ends with the Foreign Minister becoming Prime Minister and Japan helps the rest of the world. Then, there is a final epilogue showing a descendant of one of the main characters living on a space station. As they look down upon the earth, as predicted the Northern Hemisphere is covered in ice, while numerous Megafloats populate the equator.

Actually, from this concept, Komatsu even had ideas of a third part of the story which he shared on the radio program *Suntory, Saturday, and Waiting Bar* in 2006, "If I make the third part, the Japanese who lived in the second part can only go to space."

Of course, the above story was not how a 1970s *After Japan Sinks* would have unfolded as it would be set only a short time after the first film. Furthermore, it's unknown just when Komatsu got his ideas for the sequel to the novel. That being said, surely Komatsu and the other writers, whoever they may have been, would have concocted some more natural disasters to befall the world in the sequel. That was, after all, a big part of what had made the original a hit.

THE UNMADE FILES: DEEP SEA CRISIS (1974) In the Autumn of 1973, Toho smelled a hit in the form of JAPAN SINKS. They began making plans for their next great disaster film, and among the candidates were Sakyo Komatsu's DAY OF RESURRECTION (adapted by Kadokawa in 1980 and titled VIRUS for English markets) and another novel, DEEP SEA CRISIS by Takahiro Yoshimatsu. A review script for DEEP SEA CRISIS was written by Yoshimatsu and Shinichi Sekizawa by December of 1974, but the project was shelved

THE LOST FILMS FANZINE PRESENTS MOVIE MILESTONES #3

大いなる夢をSFの世界に実現！ブームの頂点を極める大作群！

●手塚治虫の畢生の大河ロマン遂に完全映画化！「永遠」は人々の心の中にある だが人類は永遠の火の鳥を求めて戦う！

火の鳥

監督■市川崑／製作■市川喜一／原作■手塚治虫
脚本■谷川俊太郎
東宝・火の鳥プロ提携／協力■東宝映画

●宇宙の洗礼を受けた人の体には青い血が流れる―今日も地球の各地で赤い血の人類の凄惨な"青血狩り"が……

UFOブルー・クリスマス

製作■嶋田親一・森岡道夫
脚本■倉本聰
東宝映画作品

●地球がひとりで生きられなくなった時 銀河宇宙の惑星たちは直径8万光年の大帝国をつくった！だがその時…

銀河帝国の攻防

製作■田中友幸・田中文雄
原作集団■小松左京・豊田有恒・高斉正・田中光二他
東宝映画作品／協力■東宝映像

●1400年間人類が追い続けた夢"ネッシー"は遂にその住家ネス湖を脱出した！北海から太平洋へ30,000浬の激闘！

ネッシー

特撮監督■中野昭慶
製作■田中友幸・イワン・ロイド・マイケル・カロラス
東宝・ハマープロ提携／協力■東宝映画

●沈みゆく列島から世界へ散った日本人3千万！迫害・紛争の中で彼等は組織化され 国土のない国家が生まれた！

続・日本沈没

原作■小松左京
製作■田中友幸
東宝映画・東宝映像提携

●ゴジラは怪獣の中の怪獣！日・米の知恵と費用をふんだんに使って描く空前の超大作！怪獣映画の新しい歴史が始まる！

日米合作 ゴジラ

製作■田中友幸
東宝映像・東宝映画
H・Gサーバーシュタイン＆アソシエーツ提携作品

THE LOST FILMS FANZINE PRESENTS MOVIE MILESTONES #3

PROPHECIES OF NOSTRADAMUS

Release Date: August 3, 1974
Alternate Titles: *The Last Days of Planet Earth* (U.S.) *The End of the World According to Nostradamus* (France) *Worldcatastrophe 1999? The Prophecies of Nostradamus* (Germany)

DIRECTED BY: Toshio Masuda SPECIAL EFFECTS BY: Teruyoshi Nakano SCREENPLAY BY: Yoshimitsu Banno & Toshio Masuda MUSIC BY: Isao Tomita CAST: Tetsuro Tamba (Dr. Ryogen Nishiyama), Kaoru Yumi (Mariko Nishiyama), Toshio Kurosawa (Akira Nakagawa), Yoko Tsukasa (Nobuo Nishiyama), So Yamamura (Prime Minister), Katsuhiko Sasaki (Nishiyama's assistant) SUIT PERFORMERS: Isamu Sugii, Nobuyuki Nakano (Soft-Bodied Humans)

Panavision, Eastmancolor, 114 Minutes

SYNOPSIS In the year 1999, the world is choked by horrible pollution. Dr. Nishiyama tries to advise the government to limit the pollution caused by factories but is unsuccessful. As the pollution worsens, strange disasters due to climate change befall the world. When a team sent to investigate a radioactive cloud over New Guinea disappears, Dr. Nishiyama volunteers to join a rescue party that goes after them, only to discover they have turned into living corpses. Back in Japan, a jet explodes and tears a hole in the ozone layer causing the countryside to erupt into flames. Then, a food shortage causes the populace to riot as the world continues to spiral out of control. In an impassioned speech, Dr. Nishiyama warns the government what will happen if they don't take precautions. During the meeting, the participants envision a world ravaged by nuclear war and inhabited by mutant survivors, and hopes that it never comes to pass.

OVERVIEW: Either hot off the success of *Submersion of Japan*, or perhaps just anticipating it, Toho intended to copy the formula for the next year's blockbuster. In this case, Tomoyuki Tanaka optioned the rights to another hit disaster book, Tsutomu "Ben" Goto's *Great Prophecies of Nostradamus*, published in November of 1973 by Shodensha. Toho had optioned the book by that December which newspapers reported on and in January, it was officially announced by Toho. (Since *Submersion of Japan* was released December 29th, it was most likely before Toho even knew for sure the film would be a hit.)

To work on the film, both as a heavily involved assistant director and script writer, Tomoyuki Tanaka turned to what some may consider an unlikely source: Yoshimitsu Banno, writer/director of the controversial *Godzilla vs.*

Yoshimitsu Banno on the set of GODZILLA VS. HEDORAH. © 1971 TOHO CO., LTD.

Hedorah (1971). Though many sources would have one believe Tanaka loathed Banno, this wasn't necessarily the case. Actually, Tanaka felt Banno had his place, it just wasn't on the Godzilla series. In fact, Hedorah's ecological horror themes are most likely what led Tanaka to entrust Banno with adapting Goto's book—which was not a novel—to film. (From the best this author can tell, Goto's book seemed to be a hypothetical scenario about what would happen to Japan if Nostradamus's predictions were to actually happen.)

Yoshimitsu Banno was instructed to adapt the book as a very loose remake of Toho's pessimistic *The Last War*, in which humanity is annihilated. (As such, that film's writer, Toshio Yasumi, gets the screenplay credit, though it was, in fact, Banno who wrote the script.) Many elements of *The Last War* are easy to spot in the form of the nuclear holocaust driven finale and main characters: a patriarch with a sick wife, his daughter, and her fiancé.

One can see Banno's handiwork all over the script as the apocalypse seems to be environmentally-driven. Experts on abnormal weather, food ecology, ultra-scientific phenomena and plant sociology were brought in to help consult. An early scene wherein children that drink from a polluted zinc mine develop strange X-Men-style abilities were based on the real-life Minamata Disaster. (People didn't develop remarkable abilities, but they were severely affected or died as a result of drinking water polluted with mercury by a nearby factory.) "I did a lot of research to write that screenplay," Banno later told Patrick Macias in *Tokyscope*. "...so I was seeing data like, one out of every four babies born in the Niigata Prefecture at the time was deformed. When that's all you're reading every day, you really start to think the world is going down the tubes, that tomorrow it will all be over." [pp.36]

Remarkably only two drafts rather than the usual four were written. As for differences, it seems Toho always had cold feet regarding the cannibalistic natives. The scene was in the first script, but was actually removed from the second and final shooting script! When it came time to actually shoot, the scene was reinstated. Also, the prime minister's speech was twice as long in the first script.

The final draft, which director Toshio

THE LOST FILMS FANZINE PRESENTS MOVIE MILESTONES #3

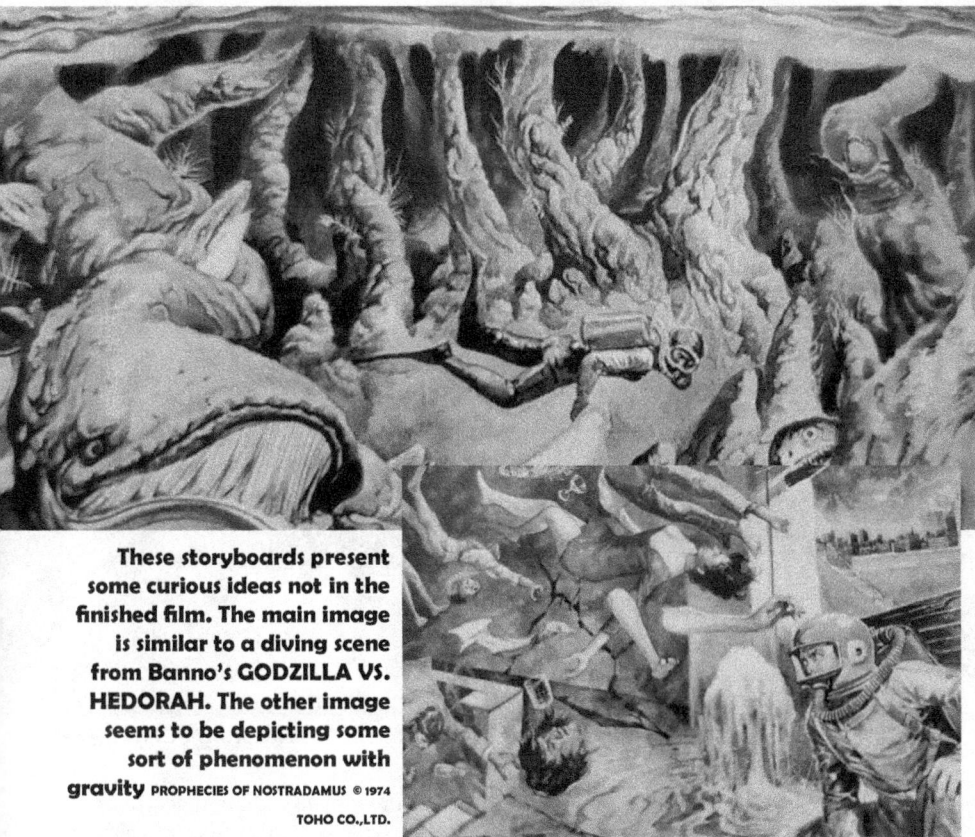

These storyboards present some curious ideas not in the finished film. The main image is similar to a diving scene from Banno's GODZILLA VS. HEDORAH. The other image seems to be depicting some sort of phenomenon with gravity. PROPHECIES OF NOSTRADAMUS © 1974 TOHO CO.,LTD.

Masuda slightly contributed to, was turned in April 30, 1974 and shooting began on May 11th with Yoshimitsu Banno heading up location shooting in New Guinea, Teruyoshi Nakano on effects, and Masuda with the main cast. The production suffered a major accident early on during filming of a scene where Tokyo oil refineries go up in an inferno because of volcanic eruptions (only a brief shot of the sequence is in the finished film as a result). The accident occurred in Studio #7 when Nakano's explosions got so out of hand that it destroyed the entire soundstage they were using, as well as the old Mogera suit from *The Mysterians* that was in storage there. By the time the Seijo Fire Department arrived, the studio had already burned down. The crew took advantage of the ruined building though, and shot footage of it as a wrecked location for the finished film! This accident occurred early on May 13th, only two days after filming began. Still, Nakano was able to finish the picture June 30th and have a test screening ready by July 24th.

The poster's tagline stated, "In 1999, all human beings will be dead. We have only 25 years of great fear remaining. This motion picture is the incredible fruit of the most advanced scientific minds and limitless imaginations." And indeed, one could well call it the ultimate disaster film. It has explosions galore, melting ice caps, mass suicides, zombies, man-eating plants, children with superpowers, massive street riots, nuclear meltdowns, cannibalism, World War III, plus giant mutated slugs, bats, and leeches. Perhaps the most amaz-

Above: Publicity still of the New Guinea sequence. Opposite Page Below: Tetsura Tamba and Toshio Kurosawa in a publicity still representing atmospheric phenomena. PROPHECIES OF NOSTRADAMUS © 1974 TOHO CO.,LTD.

ing thing about this strange milieu of disasters/phenomena is that it actually works. This is perhaps due to the fact that the film so deftly portrays a world coming apart at the seams and spiraling more and more out of control that anything seems possible. However, in this same vein, the film is comprised mostly of disastrous vignettes which naturally makes it somewhat episodic.

The New Guinea sequence (which was partially shot on location) is particularly shocking and is also one of the reasons the film eventually ended up banned—more on that later. The sequence comprises of Dr. Nishiyama and his daughter's photographer boyfriend Akira joining a U.N. mission to rescue a team of investigators that disappeared investigating a radioactive cloud over the nation. This same cloud has since mutated the local flora and fauna. Not only that, but it has also turned the natives into violent radiation-scarred cannibals. Dr. Nishiyama walks into his tent to find two of the natives literally gnawing upon a catatonic member of the expedition, blood slathered upon their maws. As the natives seem to jump from the trees and attack the camp, composer Tomita's music is excellent in the form of a primitive percussion-based track that sounds not unlike Mario Nascimbe's scores for Hammer's caveman movies of the 60s and 70s.

As the expedition members open fire on the attacking natives Dr. Nishiyama implores them to stop. That this plea was dubbed in later is a myth—Nishiyama does indeed shout out "Don't shoot! They are human beings! Don't shoot!" in the original 114-minute version as well as in the film's trailer. It would seem this was written so the following scene where Nishiyama shoots his assistant—now a zombie—to put him out of his misery, has more of an impact. After fending off the natives, the expedition finally manages to find the missing members of the first expedition. Alive yet catatonic, they sit rotting in a cave. The fact that these men are zombies (Tomita's track for this scene is even titled "Cave of the Living Dead"), and not just cannibals like the natives, is also more explicit in this version. As one of the expedition shakes his catatonic colleague's shoulder part of his rotting flesh slides off.

After this sequence ends, the narrative dissipates into a series of vignettes of various disasters. Some of the film's more striking imagery comes from a sequence where a jet fighter explodes and tears a hole in the ozone layer, causing the rays of the sun to burn people alive. In another, the polar ice caps began to melt. A scene on a backed-up Tokyo freeway with bumper-to-bumper traffic is particularly maddening in its atmosphere. Finally, an angry motorist tries to escape the freeway, which has now been backed up for several hours, and winds up crashing his car. It ignites a chain reaction with everyone else's cars and causes a huge explosion. It is one of the film's best scenes, and it was so spectacular it was trotted out again in *The War in Space* (1977), *Deathquake* (1980), *The Return of Godzilla* (1984) and *Godzilla: Final Wars* (2004). Another striking visual occurs when the smog in Tokyo gets so bad it affects the solar spectrum and turns the sky into a mirror reflecting the city's skyline.

The film's biggest shortcoming might be its final sequence, not due to what it entails, but because of a surprise twist at the last moment. In the final sequence, Dr. Nishiyama gives a speech to the Diet wherein he warns that Japan being susceptible to earthquakes and volcanoes could cause their destruction. This leads to brief stock-footage from the previous year's *Submersion of Japan* mixed in with some new effects footage as well. After this, we learn this sequence was just an example of what could happen and return to the speech, which then veers into talk of nuclear

Above: Impressive Tokyo miniature for the traffic scene. Inset: Italian poster.
PROPHECIES OF NOSTRADAMUS © 1971 TOHO CO., LTD.

war. This leads to a scene where the world is destroyed via brief clips from the very film that inspired this one: *The Last War* (1961)—the outdated miniatures sticking out like a sore thumb. However, that being said, Nakano does create some stunning new footage of nuclear missiles launching from various bases across the world.

From here, we witness the film's most controversial scene: in the aftermath of the nuclear war, two grotesquely deformed creatures that used to be humans wrestle one another over a worm crawling across the scarred earth. The scene, along with its suitmation mutants, is quite disturbing and grotesque for 1974. (The mutants, known as Soft-Bodied Humans in Japan, were designed by Toru Narita.) After the end of the world, we return to the Diet Building to learn—shock—it was all just a part of Nishiyama's speech just like the volcanoes and earthquakes from earlier (although in the Japanese and international versions, one should be tipped off as Nishiyama is narrating the entire se-

quence). As to why Toho didn't pull the trigger and let this scene be the film's real ending, the reason could be that they wanted the film to end on a note of hope in the form of the Prime Minister's speech that things can get better before destruction besets the world, but we have to work at it.

The cast is top-notch and lead by Tetsuro Tamba. His best scene occurs as he sits with his dying wife, getting so into the scene, he has a visible case of nasal drip. Well known dancer Kaoru Yumi plays his daughter Mariko. Her highlight scene occurs when she performs a dance on the beach at sunset in tribute to her mother who has just died. Toshio Kurosawa plays Akira, a photographer, and exists somewhat to be the audience's eyes and ears to witness the various disasters. This was one of Kurosawa's last films for Toho after having appeared in *The Bloodsucking Rose* the same year.

Akihiko Hirata and Hiroshi Koizumi also have small roles/cameos as two scientists. Koizumi's speech comparing the nature of rats to overpopulated humans is particularly chilling. Takashi Shimura even returns to the world of Toho SPFX films for the first time since *Frankenstein Conquers the World* (1965) as a doctor who explains to Nishiyama the recent upswing in abnormal births. As it turned out, this was Shimura's last Toho tokusatsu role.

The film was released August 3rd and grossed ¥883,000,000 making it the highest-grossing Japanese film of 1974. This isn't surprising considering that audiences were hungry for another big disaster film after the success of *Submersion of Japan*. As stated before, the fantastic film is full of visuals such as bizarre storms, the disastrous car pileup in Tokyo, massive flooding, and forest fires caused by a hole in the ozone layer. The ending scene with the two mutated humans wrestling in a post-apocalyptic wasteland is where the trouble started, as the post-apocalyptic mutants were deemed by some to be offensive to Hiroshima survivors.

A Bomb Sufferers Organizations Council and the No Nukes Group from Osaka Prefecture went to the Eirin Board (the Japanese equivalent of the MPAA) and demanded Toho stop screening the film. One week after release, Toho ran newspaper ads apologizing for the content of the film. They pulled the movie and recut it down to 90 minutes to remove the offensive footage. For international markets, however, the offensive scenes still remained and the film was retitled *Prophecies of Nostradamus (Catastrophe 1999)*, though this version still ran at 90 minutes.

1980 was the last time that the uncut version was legally screened when it was broadcast as TV Asahi's "Holiday Special" at 7:00 PM on November 3rd. *Prophecies of Nostradamus (Catastrophe 1999)* played in New York and Los Angeles theaters in 1978 (where it was reviewed by the *Los Angeles Times* as well as an unidentified New York newspaper). In 1981, it was released to American TV by United Productions of America as the heavily recut *The Last Days of Planet Earth* and in 1995 this version was released to VHS by Paramount Home Video. This is the only licensed home video release in America, and the film has never been released in Japan in any format (the recut 90 minute Japanese version is occasionally screened in revivals, though). The movie has been released in Europe (chiefly Denmark, Germany, Italy, and France) on VHS in varying editions.

Yoshimitsu Banno told Damon Foster in an interview that, "This is a movie that's essentially banned in Japan. As I understand it, that came about because some protest groups, just after the movie was released, rallied against it because they didn't agree with the portrayal of nuclear war survivors as mutants. So Toho put a self-imposed ban on it and will not have anything to do with it anymore."

Hopefully one day in the future, Toho will see fit to release this rare classic, seen by very few in all of its intended uncut apocalyptic glory.

**Opposite Page: Publicity still.
This Page: Various behind-the-scenes stills.**
PROPHECIES OF NOSTRADA-
MUS © 1974 TOHO CO., LTD.

THE LOST FILMS FANZINE PRESENTS MOVIE MILESTONES #3

Right: Do the giant slugs in **PROPHECIES OF NOSTRADAMUS** count as kaiju? Who can say, but they certainly are gigantic for their species.

PROPHECIES OF NOSTRADAMUS © 1974 TOHO CO.,LTD.

THE LOST FILMS FANZINE PRESENTS MOVIE MILESTONES #3

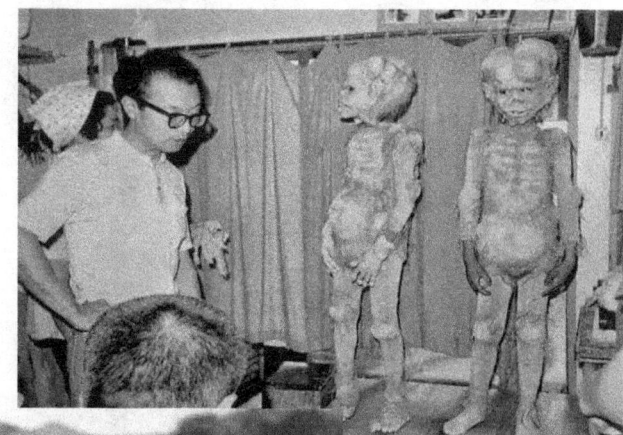

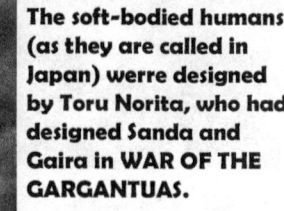

The soft-bodied humans (as they are called in Japan) werre designed by Toru Norita, who had designed Sanda and Gaira in WAR OF THE GARGANTUAS.

PROPHECIES OF NOSTRADAMUS © 1974 TOHO CO.,LTD.

79

This manga version of PROPHECIES OF NOSTRADAMUS was published in the September 1974 issue of BESSATSU SHONEN CHAMPION. It was written by Professor Yoshisato Takayama, who was prominent in the "Shonen Jump" of the 1970s. It ran at 49 large pages and was faithful to the film, outside of over dramatizing a few things like the giant carnivorous plant. PROPHECIES OF NOSTRADAMUS © 1974 TOHO CO.,LTD.

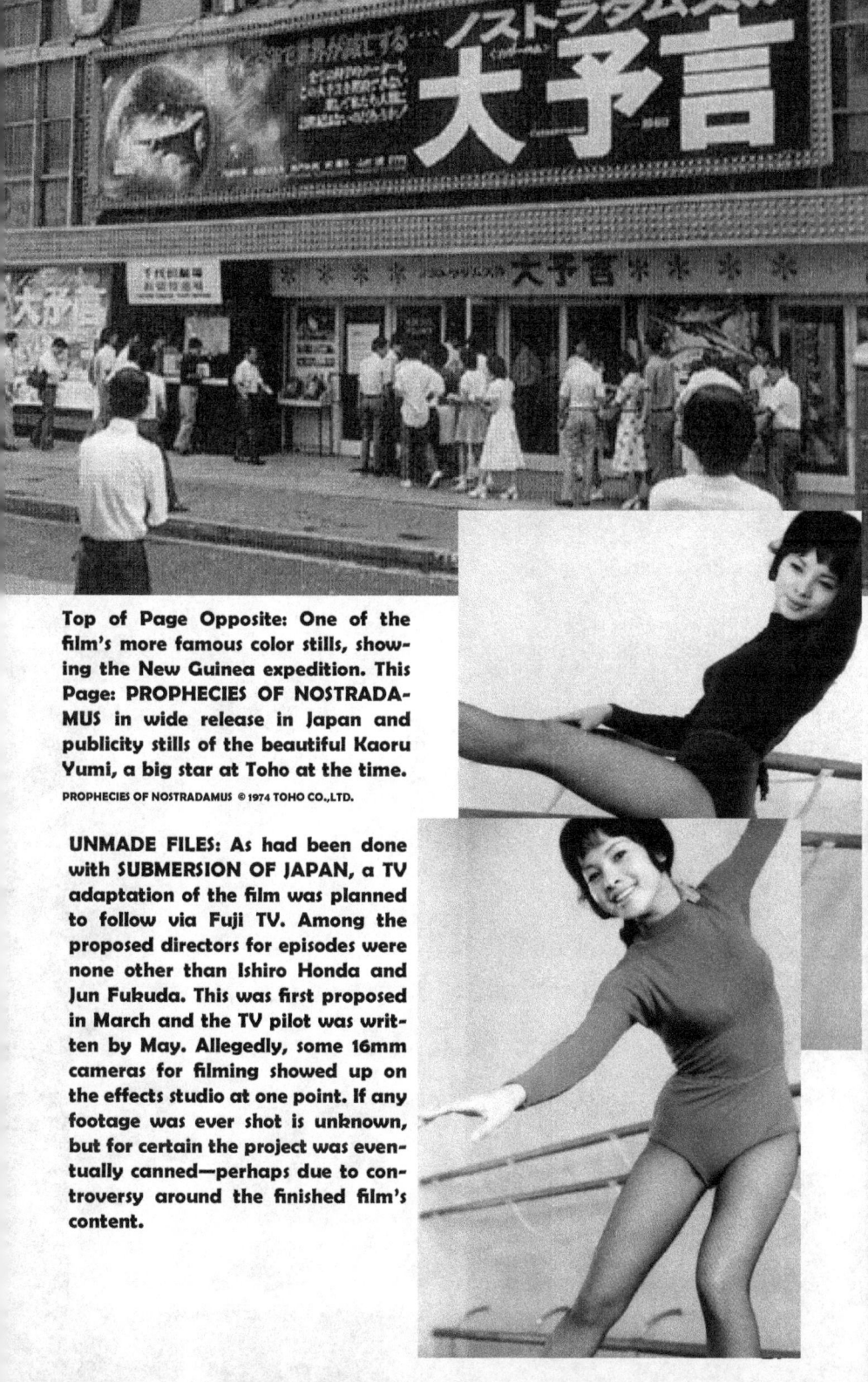

Top of Page Opposite: One of the film's more famous color stills, showing the New Guinea expedition. This Page: PROPHECIES OF NOSTRADAMUS in wide release in Japan and publicity stills of the beautiful Kaoru Yumi, a big star at Toho at the time.

PROPHECIES OF NOSTRADAMUS © 1974 TOHO CO.,LTD.

UNMADE FILES: As had been done with **SUBMERSION OF JAPAN**, a TV adaptation of the film was planned to follow via Fuji TV. Among the proposed directors for episodes were none other than Ishiro Honda and Jun Fukuda. This was first proposed in March and the TV pilot was written by May. Allegedly, some 16mm cameras for filming showed up on the effects studio at one point. If any footage was ever shot is unknown, but for certain the project was eventually canned—perhaps due to controversy around the finished film's content.

その時、人類は…

恐怖の「グランドクロス」が引き起こす人類滅亡のスペクタクル
前作をさらに上回る大スケールで描くスペクタクル巨編

1999

原作 五島 勉　製作 田中友幸　監督 舛田利雄

ノストラダムスの大予言Ⅱ
恐怖の大魔王

1975年7の月、公開決定！

Page Opposite: Ad for the unmade sequel. Above: Publicity still from PROPHECIES OF NOSTRADAMUS depicting the jet that explodes and burns a hole in the ozone layer. PROPHECIES OF NOSTRADAMUS © 1974 TOHO CO.,LTD.

THE UNMADE FILES: GREAT PROPHECIES OF NOSTRADAMUS II: FEAR OF THE GREAT DEVIL (1975) This sequel to GREAT PROPHECIES OF NOSTRADAMUS, the most successful film of 1974, was initially set for release in 1975. Meant to be comprised of the same production crew as the first film, it was likely cancelled due to trouble caused by the "No Nukes" group in regard to the first film. The unfinished story treatment (the story concept of which was said to be created by Tomoyuki Tanaka) tells of reporter Tsutomu Goto (named after the real writer of the book which the screenplay for GREAT PROPHECIES OF NOSTRADAMUS was based upon) investigating an experiment in East Asia using spirit mediums in an attempt to contact the long dead Nostradamus about his predictions concerning the end of the world. As seen in the previous film, the world is consumed in a global conflict, with the battles taking place on land, at sea, under the sea, and even in outer space. At the end, a huge U.F.O. appears over Japan, the one nation to stay neutral while the rest of the world was at war. Though the U.F.O. is regarded as the great King of Terror that falls from the sky in Nostradamus's prophecies, the U.F.O. takes the Japanese people into space to begin a new future while the world burns. Also attached to this project was writer Masato Ide, author of screenplays for Akira Kurosawa films such as RED BEARD (1965). Fourteen pages were written for this treatment in all. On a related note, in 1991, Tsutomu Goto finally published a sequel to his original book entitled PREDICTIONS OF NOSTRADAMUS: MIDDLE EAST CHAPTER

SAKYO KOMATSU'S

SYNOPSIS: Yoshio Tamura and Maria Harada are two of the top members of ESPY, a secret government agency comprised of psychic spies. To stop an assassination attempt on the Bulgarian Prime Minister by the evil Counter-ESPY ran by Ulrov, they recruit the help of psychic race car driver Jiro Miki. It is Ulrov's hope that the assassination will incite World War III, and to deal with the agents of ESPY, he sends psychic assassin Goro Tatsumi to take care of them.

ESPY

Release Date: December 28, 1974
Alternate Titles: *E.S.P./Spy* (U.S.) *ESPY* (1974)

DIRECTED BY: Jun Fukuda SPECIAL EFFECTS BY: Teruyoshi Nakano SCREENPLAY BY: Ei Ogawa MUSIC BY: Masaru Sato CAST: Hiroshi Fujioka (Yoshio Tamura), Kaoru Yumi (Maria Harada), Masao Kusakari (Jiro Miki), Tomisaburo Wakayama (Ulrov), Katsumasa Uchida (Goro Tatsumi), Yuzo Kayama (Hojo), Goro Mutsumi (Teraoka), Eiji Okada (Salabad), Andrew Hughes (ESPY Int. Manager)

Tohoscope, Eastmancolor, 94 Minutes

PSYCHIC SPIES

After defeating Tatsumi and thwarting the assassination via Yoshio's new ability to teleport, together the trio track Ulrov to his castle where he is defeated once and for all.

OVERVIEW: Due to *Submersion of Japan's* success, Toho was hot to adapt another Sakyo Komatsu property. In this case, Toho turned to a film they had planned to produce seven years ago but had abandoned: *ESPY*. Komatsu's *Esupai* (or a spy with ESP) had begun as a manga in *Weekly Manga Sunday* in 1964. The film rights had been acquired by Toho in February of 1966 and was announced for production soon after. Even back then, Jun Fukuda was to direct the movie based upon a script written by Ei Ogawa.

It seems the 1966 iteration of *ESPY* (eyed for a 1967 release) was in part inspired by the huge James Bond/spy craze of the late 1960s. In fact, the original *ESPY* was to have starred Akiko Wakabayashi (Aki, the ill-fated Bond girl in *You Only Live Twice*), along with Tatsuya Mihashi (1970's *Tora! Tora! Tora!* and "Phil Moscowitz" in Woody Allen's *What's Up Tiger Lily?*), Makoto Sato (Uchida in *The H-Man*), and Mie Hama (Madame Piranha in *King Kong Escapes* and Kissy Suzuki in *You Only Live Twice*). However, Wakabayashi left Toho, which already had a busy year in 1967, and they shelved the film. The final nail in the coffin came with the launching of the U.S./Japanese co-production of *Latitude Zero*, which turned into a disaster from start to finish.

Submersion's massive success had reminded Toho that they already owned the rights to another Komatsu story, but that wasn't the only reason the script was revived. "There was a great deal of interest in E.S.P. in the early 1970s. That also prompted Toho to produce *ESPY* when it did," Fumio Tanaka told David Milner. A visit to Japan by famed psychic Uri Geller in 1974 also ignited a fire under Toho. "I remember that the pages of the screenplay were already beginning to turn yellow when I read [the script]," Tanaka said.

Toei's Masahiro Kakefuda (author of Toho's soon-to-be-aborted *The Human Torch*) was commissioned to update the script in 1974. Whatever Kakefuda's update entailed, it was apparently unsatisfactory as original writer Ei Ogawa was called in to overhaul Kakefuda's take. Fumio Tanaka revealed that budgetary constraints forced the following change to be made: "...The hideout of the villain originally was going to be a satellite in orbit instead of a mansion in the mountains." Oddly, this satellite remains on the release poster! Furthermore, in the original script from 1967, the villain Ulrov was an alien that lived on a satellite which lead ESPY Tamura would teleport himself to for the end showdown. Tomoyuki Tanaka himself stepped in to cut this aspect. Yet, there's an odd, throwaway line at the end of the finished film that alludes to Ulrov being possessed by some evil power "not of this earth"! An alternative story says that in one draft of the script Ulrov's base was located on the moon—an idea that Teruyoshi Nakano nixed himself.

Some of the character names were

Above: ESPY's cast (from left to right): Masao Kusakari, Hiroshi Fujioka, Yuzo Kayama and Kaoru Yumi. Inset: Jun Fukuda (second from right) with the cast. ESPY © 1974 TOHO CO.,LTD.

changed from the manga with Maria Tosti becoming Maria Harada. Added into the film version was a character that didn't appear in the manga or the 1967 script: Jiro Miki—a race car driver. Originally the character was to be a college student but someone decided race car driver would be more interesting. Ulrov transitioned from an alien to an ESP-enhanced human bent on avenging the death of his father by causing WWIII. Originally, Ulrov was named Linz (who claimed to have the abilities of Buddha) and came from Armenia. The prime minister in Ulrov's crosshairs was not from the fictional country of Baltonia but China. The final draft was reportedly very close to the finished film and the only notable scene cut was Ulrov executing one of his operatives, Judy, inside his western-style estate. This tracks since in the finished film, Judy just mysteriously disappears. Another cut scene would have featured actress Linda Blair. While promoting The Exorcist in Japan in July of 1974, Toho reached out to her with an offer to appear in the film. Blair was interested, but her agent advised her against it.

It's possible Masahiro Kakefuda recycled some elements from his abandoned script, The Human Torch, when it came time to bring Ulrov's outer space lair down to earth. Much of The Human Torch revolves around a large, western-gothic style estate where a pyrotechnic being runs amok. Considering Ulrov resides in what is more or less a medieval mansion and meets his death by catching fire, the odds favor *Human Torch* inspiring the revised climax of *ESPY*.

The resulting film is reminiscent of a James Bond movie, right down to an ambitious pre-credit scene where Katsumasa Uchida (Murakoshi in *Terror of Mechagodzilla*) uses his psychic abilities to assassinate four delegates on a train rushing through Switzerland. The globetrotting doesn't stop at Switzerland; on location-filmed action scenes take place in Paris and Turkey as well. The Turkey sequence contains a notorious striptease where Maria is hypnotized into dancing. When she is approached by one of Ulrov's henchmen, Yoshio psychically rips his tongue out in a scene cut for the U.S. TV version aired years later in the 1980s (which ruins the continuity of the film in later scenes).

The highlight of the film for many special effects buffs occurs when a jumbo jet (piloted by *Godzilla vs. Megalon's* Robert Dunham) is psychically induced to crash into some mountains before Yoshio takes the controls and saves the day. Fans of Teruyoshi Nakano may notice that his rocky landscape used for the plane scene is awfully familiar to the Siberia set, sans the snow, used in the same year's *Godzilla vs. Mechagodzilla* and could have been the same set only redressed. The film's climax, where Yoshio gains the ability to teleport just as the car he is trapped in explodes, is also well edited and exciting.

ESPY was another hit for Toho, coming in at #2 behind *Prophecies of Nostradamus* for the title of top-grossing Japanese film of 1974. The film's success wasn't surprising at all; *ESPY* is a fast-paced action thriller clearly modeled after the James Bond series. Overall, the idea of spies with psychic powers is utilized quite well throughout the film. However, even though audiences enjoyed the film, Komatsu was reportedly not pleased with it.

Below: Stills from one of ESPY's more notorious scenes. ESPY © 1974 TOHO CO., LTD.

THE LOST FILMS FANZINE PRESENTS MOVIE MILESTONES #3

BULLET TRAIN

Release Date: July 5, 1975
Japanese Title: *Shinkansen Explosion*

DIRECTED BY: Junya Satō SCREENPLAY BY: Ryūnosuke Ono, Junya Satō & Ari Katō (story) MUSIC BY: Hachirô Aoyama CAST: Ken Takakura (Tetsuo Okita), Sonny Chiba (Aoki), Ken Utsui (Kuramochi), Fumio Watanabe (Miyashita), Kei Yamamoto (Masaru Koga), Eiji Gō (Shinji Fujio), Akira Oda (Hiroshi Ōshiro), Yasuhiro Aoki (Officer Senda), Yumiko Fujita (Akiyama), Tetsurō Tamba (Sunaga)

Toeiscope, Color, 152 Minutes

SYNOPSIS Tetsuo Okita is a down on his luck businessman who's just lost his manufacturing company. To try and make ends meet, he teams with two other men to extort money from the Japanese government. Okita places a unique bomb on the Hikari 109 bullet train that becomes activated once the train exceeds 80kph. By the same token, if the speed drops below 80kph, the bomb will detonate. Okita demands $5 million for instructions to dismantle the bomb. The government pays up, and unfortunately, the location where Okita left the instructions burns up in an unrelated fire. Okita has also become increasingly difficult to trace as he runs from the police. Eventually, investigators determine the location of the bomb. The conductor, Aoki, uses a welding torch to cut into the floor and disarm the bomb, saving the train. This is not reported to the press, however, and a fake plea for help goes out to Okita over the airwaves. Okita calls the officials one last time to tell them how to dismantle the bomb. In doing so, he is tracked by the police to Haneda Airport where he is shot and killed.

OVERVIEW: Of all the Japanese Panic Movies ever produced, 1975's *Bullet Train* probably has the most in common with an American disaster movie. This shouldn't come as a surprise as Toei President Shigeru Okada cited American movies like *The Towering Inferno* as this one's inspiration (though surely Toho's mega-hits *Submersion of Japan* and *Prophecies of Nostradamus* didn't go unnoticed).

The production of a Toei Panic Movie was greenlit at a May 1974 meeting. However, before deciding upon the runaway train, Toei first had ideas of producing their own version of *The Towering Inferno* to star Sonny Chiba. The

THE LOST FILMS FANZINE PRESENTS MOVIE MILESTONES #3

Ken Takakura as Tetsuo Okita in BULLET TRAIN. BULLET TRAIN © 1975 TOEI CO.,LTD.

project was called *36th Floor Burning* and was apparently similar to the movie *Backdraft*, produced in 1991. Though the project was reported in the papers, it was never filmed. Instead, someone within Toei's planning department had seen a screenplay written by Akira Kurosawa about a runaway train. While Toei didn't film it (Cannon produced the film *Runaway Train* in 1985 starring Jon Voight, actually), they did take inspiration from it. In this case, they decided it would be interesting if the threat revolved around a Shinkansen bullet train that couldn't stop. Specifically, a bomb would be planted on the train, and once it gets going it can't drop its speed below 80 kph. (If that sounds just like 1994's better-known *Speed*, that's because supposedly this film inspired *Speed*.)

While this film may have inspired *Speed*, it was itself inspired by 1970's *Airport*, wherein an airliner can't land for the threat of a bomb on board. Essentially, Toei writers took that idea, injected the speed elements, and put the scenario on a bullet train. At first, the film was titled *Chase the Shinkansen Bombing Devil* but was eventually shortened to *Shinkansen Bombing* (*Bullet Train* internationally). Before shooting commenced, Toei tried to obtain the cooperation of the Japanese National Railways (JNR), as filming would be difficult without them. This proved to be frustrating, as the JNR feared that the film's scenario would inspire copycats, not to mention the fact that JNR routinely received many false bomb threats already. (JNR also disliked the title and suggested that it be changed to the less lethal sounding *Shinkansen Crisis Close Call*!) Ultimately, JNR refused to cooperate with Toei, and so the studio turned to special effects to bring their train to life for the most part. Two different miniature trains were built (each at a cost of 20 million yen). The train cars of each were one meter long, with twelve cars on each total. These were then put on a 50 meter long track, so a lot of work

THE LOST FILMS FANZINE PRESENTS MOVIE MILESTONES #3

Tetsuo Okita and his two criminal comrades in BULLET TRAIN. BULLET TRAIN © 1975 TOEI CO.,LTD.

went into them! (Reportedly, some of the miniatures were later recycled in the 1980 TV series *Ultraman 80*).

Once it was determined how to bring the real star of the movie to life (the train itself) Toei could then go onto casting the "secondary players". Notably, *Bullet Train* involves more of an all-star cast than Toho's recent panic movies did, and the revolving door of big time stars included Ken Takakura, Sonny Chiba, and Tetsuro Tamba. However, only Takakura really gets the limelight and has the most screen time as the thief, Tetsuo Okita. The character is the focal point of the story (depending upon which version of the film you watch) and is easily the story's best character. However, it wasn't always this way, and apparently before Takakura was cast, the character was more one-dimensional and less sympathetic. But, upon his casting, he was given a backstory, hence the flashbacks involving his character (which were cut out of the more widely seen international version of the film).

Sonny Chiba is only significant as the train conductor, Aoki, in the first act and the last act—we hardly see him during the movie's middle portion. According to production notes, Chiba was originally cast in a different role but switched to the part of Aoki later (it was also Chiba's idea that he be the one to disarm the bomb).

Lastly, Tetsuro Tamba is noted as a guest star and hardly has any screen time at all. On the note of Tamba, thanks to *Submersion* and *Nostradamus*, he had more or less established himself as the actor most identified with the panic film genre by this point. Tamba isn't the only actor recognizable from Toho sci-fi; many Godzilla series stars pop up in *Bullet Train* as well. The great Takashi Shimura (Dr. Yamane in 1954's *Godzilla*) has a small role, as does Yutaka Hayashi (Jinkawa in 1973's God*zilla vs. Megalon*). Sharp-eyed viewers will also notice plenty of other Toho bit players in the background as well.

And how does *Bullet Train* stack up in the pantheon of Panic Films? Its production qualities are top-notch all around, from the direction to the music and the acting. However, it just doesn't capture the same mood as *Submersion of Japan*, which will always be the seminal Japanese panic movie. How well *Bullet Train* stacks up again *Prophecies of Nostradamus* is debatable, though sci-fi and effects fans will no doubt prefer *PoN*. *Bullet Train* is probably most comparable to that same year's *Conflagration*. Like that film, *Bullet Train* faced the tough decision between stopping the disaster before it can occur (blowing up the train) or showing the disaster occur. Naturally, if audiences don't see any exploding trains and carnage they might feel cheated. At the same time, the train blowing up would also mean that the heroes had failed. And so Toei compromised by showing the explosion as an imagined simulation in the minds of several characters. (Toho would more or less do the same thing in *Conflagration*, but did a slightly better job of it.)

Budgeted at 530 million yen, the film began shooting in the spring of 1975 and was released that summer going up against Toho's *Conflagration*. However, it was tough in getting the film to theaters as the JNR tried their best to get Toei to shelve the film and not release it at all! JNR pulled some strings that at least inhibited Toei's advertising methods for the film, and as such, when it was released it was not a hit in Japan. The film was successfully exported to many other countries, however, where it did slightly better.

UNMADE FILES: Before **BULLET TRAIN**, Akira Kurosawa almost made his own train-disaster movie. In 1963 he had read an article LIFE MAGAZINE about a runaway train and he thought it would make a good movie. He then contacted Joseph E. Levine (the U.S. producer of 1956's **GODZILLA, KING OF THE MONSTERS**) about doing an international co-production. Levine agreed, and in June of 1966 Kurosawa announced the co-production with Levine's Embassy Pictures. The budget was set at $5.6 million and the script was written by Kurosawa, Hideo Oguni and Ryuzo Kikushima. Their story concerned two escaped convicts who hide on board a stationary train, which then rolls away gradually picking up more and more speed. The plan was to shoot the film in 70 mm along tracks between Syracuse and Rochester in New York over 16 weeks in October of 1966. Unfortunately, the production was cancelled at the last minute with plans to resume production at a later date, which never came. By April of 1967 the film had been "indefinitely postponed" and Kurosawa became distracted with **TORA! TORA! TORA!** The film was eventually produced and released by Cannon in 1985.

THE LOST FILMS FANZINE PRESENTS MOVIE MILESTONES #3

THE LOST FILMS FANZINE PRESENTS MOVIE MILESTONES #3

BULLET TRAIN © 1975 TOEI CO., LTD.

THE LOST FILMS FANZINE PRESENTS MOVIE MILESTONES #3

CONFLAGRATION

Release Date: July 12, 1975
Alternate Titles: *Tokyo Bay Burns* (Japan) *High-Seas Hijack* (U.S.) *Explosion* (Italy) *Steel Inferno* (Finland) *Attacked by the Colossus of the Seas* (Peru) *The Ocean on Fire* (Spain) *Big Alarm in Tokyo Bay* (Sweden) *Hell Journey into the Unknown* (Germany)

DIRECTED BY: Katsumune Ishida SPECIAL EFFECTS BY: Teruyoshi Nakano SCREENPLAY BY: Toshio Masuda, Yasuko Ōno, & Koji Tanaka (novel) MUSIC BY: Hajime Kaburagi CAST: Tetsuro Tamba (Captain Munekata), Hiroshi Fujioka (Yakatajiro), K. Amoha (Simba), Willie Dorsey (Zamba), Mizuho Suzuki (Katsuragi), Dai Kanai (Dr. Hatsuyama), Midori Kanazawa (Michiko)

Tohoscope, Color, 100 Minutes

SYNOPSIS Japanese oil tanker the *Arabian Light* is bound for Tokyo Bay when it picks up a band of shipwreck survivors in a life raft. The crew immediately learns the men are actually terrorists who almost immediately take over the ship. The terrorists hide a bomb on board the vessel, the plan being to sail it into Tokyo Bay and then detonate it unless the Japanese themselves blow up the Kiyama CTS oil reserve. In that case, the terrorists will disarm the bombs and let the hostages go. The Japanese government gets the idea to get Toho to stage a special effects scene depicting the fake destruction of Kiyama and broadcast it on live television. The government implements the risky plan and all goes well until it suddenly begins to rain, cluing the terrorists in that it's all being staged. The crew finally gets sick of being held hostage and revolts. Their captain is killed but so are the terrorists. With help from the government, the *Arabian Light's* first mate is able to discover the bomb moments before it explodes.

OVERVIEW: Naturally, after two back-to-back panic films, Toho had desires of filming a third. Had there not been a great controversy regarding *Great Prophecies of Nostradamus*, Toho's big summer disaster film would have likely been *Great Prophecies of Nostradamus II: Fear of the Great Devil*. Instead, Toho's next disaster film would end up being far more grounded in reality than either *Great Prophecies of Nostradamus* or *Submersion of Japan* had been. The new film would be based around an oil tanker disaster, a concept based on both a real event and a novel. The aforementioned event was an oil tanker disaster that occurred in Tokyo Bay in November of 1974 when an oil tanker and a cargo ship collided. The novel, *Critical*

The huge Arabian Light model in a publicity still. CONFLAGRATION © 1975 TOHO CO.,LTD.

Explosion—which the film follows—was by Koji Tanaka, a prolific Japanese writer who was just starting his career. As with the two previous disaster films, Osamu Tanaka produced alongside Tomoyuki Tanaka.

The effects portion of the film, *Conflagration* (*Tokyo Bay Burns* in its native Japan), was limited compared to the preceding disaster films. The oil tanker miniature was quite large at 7.2 meters and was designed by Yasuyuki Inoue of the art department. Teruyoshi Nakano's explosion scenes were so good that they seamlessly blended in as stock footage in no less than three Godzilla movies: *Godzilla vs. King Ghidorah* (1991), *Godzilla Against Mechagodzilla* (2002) and *Godzilla: Final Wars* (2004).

Naturally, location shooting was done with the cast on a real tanker owned by Mitsui OSK Lines, Ltd. However, for safety's sake, filming was done on days when the ship was loaded with ore rather than flammable liquids.

Conflagration is a different, more grounded affair than its two panic movie predecessors with no sci-fi elements at all. However, as a disaster film that revolves around stopping the disaster rather than showcasing it outright, *Conflagration* is one of those films that struggles with having its cake and eating it too. On one hand, if the destruction isn't prevented, then the protagonists of the film have failed. On the other, if the destruction of Tokyo Bay isn't shown, then the audience will be very, very disappointed. To accomplish this task, the destruction of Tokyo Bay is shown as a simulation in the minds of the government. Later, there is a sequence where a film crew tries to trick the terrorists with a miniature explosion of the Kiyama Oil Fields—more or less the main setpiece of the film. The two explosion simulation scenes are very well done in the hands of "Mr. Explosion" Teruyoshi Nakano (whom an expy of is hauled in to create the Kiyama miniature explosions). The first simulation, which occurs thirty minutes into the film, shows what would happen if the tanker landed in Tokyo Bay, with gallons of oil spilling into the water. Fumes from the oil then kill hundreds in Tokyo, and a jumbo jet that flies over the city even explodes in midair. The staged special effects scene in the third act is well directed from a dramatic standpoint. All is going well and the terrorists, watching a TV on the ship, are fooled until it begins to rain. The problem occurs because the television director is using a split-screen technique of the real oil fields, where it unexpectedly begins to rain, and the fake, miniature reproduction. One half of the screen shows a clear sky, while the other half shows rain. The jig is up, and the crew must then find a way to stop the terrorists on their own.

The film is carried by Toho's two reigning panic film champions: Hiroshi Fujioka (*Submersion of Japan*) and Tetsuro Tamba, who pulled disaster double duty that year when he also starred in Toei's *The Bullet Train*. The film is loaded with the usual 1970's tropes, such as having Fujioka's character flashback to slow-motion scenes of he and his girlfriend frolicking in and out of the bedroom. He and Tamba deliver the usual solid performances, but the film is mired by the villains, who lack a good command of the English and Japanese languages of which, the majority of their dialogue is spoken. A *Die Hard* Hans Gruber-like villain anchoring the film would have benefited it greatly, though the main villain does get one lengthy scene where he and Tamba discuss the moral ethics of what he is trying to accomplish. Fujioka gets more to do than Tamba in several good action scenes fighting the terrorists. Fujioka kills the final terrorist by shooting him with a spear gun after Tamba's character has valiantly died. Fujioka then has to go scuba diving in the ship's gasoline reservoir to find the bomb, which he removes in the nick of time. It would seem that Toho's third disaster film of the seventies failed to excite at the box office though and a planned second entry in their new "panic film" series failed to materialize.

Like *Submersion of Japan/Tidal Wave*, this film was also picked up and re-edited by an American distributor, in this case Cinema Producer's Alliance and Pine Productions. The added subplots are completely unnecessary but it is at least better handled than the new footage in *Tidal Wave*. Furthermore, with *Conflagration* being only 100 minutes vs. *Submersion of Japan's* two-plus hours, *Conflagration* was a much easier film to edit down. This time, the American TV actor chosen to lead the film was Peter Graves, best known at the time for *Mission: Impossible*. In the film's most meta moment, in one of the added scenes, the lady reporter character catches on that it was Toho Studios who handled the simulated explosion (the same thing happens in the Japanese version with its male reporter equivalent character. They both even claim to have seen the footage last year while covering the filming of "Earth 1999")! This U.S. version of *Conflagration* was retitled *High-Seas Hijack* and released in 1978.

THE LOST FILMS FANZINE PRESENTS MOVIE MILESTONES #3

Several international posters and various behind the scenes stills of the expansive miniatures for the ARABIAN LIGHT and the Kiyama oil fields.
CONFLAGRATION © 1975 TOHO CO., LTD.

THE UNMADE FILES

GREAT EVACUATION (1976) Based upon a 1975 novel by Koji Tanaka, the film adaptation had a screenplay by Shuichi Nagahara (1977's THE WAR IN SPACE) and was to be directed by Toshio Masuda (1974's GREAT PROPHECIES OF NOSTRADAMUS). The film was to be the second entry in Toho's "Special Effects Panic Movie" series to follow 1975's CONFLAGRATION. GREAT EVACUATION would have seen a passenger plane crash land on a deserted island. However, the island is a secret testing ground for biological weapons. Eventually, the main character (a photographer named Ryuzaki) is the only survivor and is pursued by a faction of the Japanese government that wants to keep the island a secret. Had the film been made, it would have predated movies such as VIRUS (1980) and OUTBREAK (1995). In 1983, the script was adapted into a manga.

NOBORU TSUBURAYA'S UNTITLED DISASTER MOVIE (1978) More of a desire than an actual, bonafide project; Noboru Tsuburaya stated that one day he dreamed of doing a disaster movie similar to Irwin Allen films such as THE POSEIDON ADVENTURE (1972) or THE TOWERING INFERNO (1974). Specifically, Tsuburaya was speaking about the success of working on THE LAST DINOSAUR for ABC in 1978: "We've reached the top of Mont-Blanc (the ABC television network), now we'd like to climb Everest (Irwin Allen disaster films)." This statement was taken from the JAPANESE FANTASY FILM JOURNAL #12, which itself is quoting from a February 6, 1977 article from the SAN FRANCISCO EXAMINER AND CHRONICLE.

LEGEND OF DINOSAURS AND MONSTER BIRDS

Release Date: April 29, 1977
Alternate Titles: *Legend of Dinosaurs and Ominous Birds* (Japan) *The "Legend of Dinosaurs"* (U.S.) *Giants of the Past* (Germany) *The Monsters of Prehistory* (France) *Earthquake 10* (Italy) *Legend of Dinosaurs* (Russia)

DIRECTED BY: Junji Kurata SPECIAL EFFECTS BY: Fuminori Obayashi SCREENPLAY BY: Isao Matsumoto & Ichiro Otsu MUSIC BY: Masao Yagi CAST: Tsunehiko Watase (Ashizawa), Nobiko Sawa (Akiko), Tomoko Kiyoshima (Junko), Shotako Hayashi (Akira), Fuyukichi Maki (Muku)

Toeiscope, Color, 92 Minutes

THE LOST FILMS FANZINE PRESENTS MOVIE MILESTONES #3

The most famous scene in LEGEND OF DINOSAURS & MONSTER BIRDS. © 1977 TOEI CO.,LTD.

SYNOPSIS An ice cave full of prehistoric eggs is rumored to lie beneath the forests of Mt. Fuji which brings Tokyo geologist Ashizawa to the area. During his investigation, Ashizawa meets an old flame, Akiko, a photographer scuba diving in Lake Sai with her friend Junko. It becomes apparent that something is lurking in the waters after several mysterious deaths occur including Junko's. Soon Lake Sai is besieged by scientific equipment and investigators who have no luck in finding the monster, alleged to be a Plesiosaurus. In the ice cave, one of the eggs hatches a Rhamphorynchus that kills two spelunkers. Determined to see the dinosaur in the lake for himself, Ashizawa and Akiko go scuba diving. With no luck finding the monster, they travel up an underwater passage into the ice cave where they find the broken egg and the grizzly remains of the two victims. Back on the surface, the newly-hatched Rhamphorynchus kills several of the town's populace and then returns to the forest.

Making their way outside the cave, Ashizawa and Akiko are shocked to see the Plesiosaur roaming the woods. Soon it battles the returning Rhamphorynchus as Mt. Fuji begins to erupt. The Plesiosaurus is killed when it falls into a fissure caused by the massive eruption. Ashizawa and Akiko's fate is unclear, though they are at least together.

OVERVIEW: Although *Jaws* isn't thought of as a "disaster movie" in the U.S., Japan labeled the film as an "Animal Panic Movie." And with that little loophole in mind, I present to you Toei's *Legend of Dinosaurs and Monster Birds*. Though usually labeled as a monster movie, I would consider it a Panic Movie. As it is, the story is as much about Mt. Fuji's impending eruption as it is the dinosaurs. Said eruption is also what caps off the story, but we're getting ahead of ourselves.

The movie began life a bit more similar to *Jaws*, as the unspecified aquatic dinosaur lived in the ocean rather than a lake, and stalked the shores of a Jap-

99

anese island, Kisogashima. (As to why Toei simply didn't do their own shark movie, they may have chosen a plesiosaur because Toho was planning to do a movie about the Loch Ness Monster at the time.)

Even though it does feature a plesiosaur rather than a shark, there are naturally plenty of callbacks to *Jaws* (such as a shark fin hoax, a town meeting where someone draws the monster on a chalkboard, etc.) The film also tipped its hat to another popular 'Animal Panic Movie,' that being *Grizzly*. That film had several POV shots of the bear stalking victims in the woods, and this film does the same with dinosaurs. Throughout the film, characters predict that the emergence of dinosaurs will cause an earthquake (for whatever reason). As stated earlier, the film ends with Mt. Fuji erupting. The long sequence sees the two romantic leads reaching for one another over a chasm that's opened in the earth, and it would seem the scene was inspired by the *Submersion of Japan* TV series final scene.

Though Toei had hoped that this film would see distribution in 40 countries (including America) it was a failure at the Japanese box office. However, it was a massive success in, of all places, the Soviet Union. The film was heavily re-edited for its Italian release, which rebranded it as a straight disaster movie called *Terremoto 10 Grado* (or, *Magnitude 10 Earthquake* to capitalize off of *Earthquake's* success in Italy). The wild re-edit added in a subplot about an asteroid hitting a satellite, and it also illegally replaced the original score with John Barry's excellent tracks from 1977's *The Deep*!

Legend of Dinosaurs wound up going straight to U.S. television in 1983 and later to home video under King Features' "Just For Kids!" label, which cut much of the violence, making many scenes in the film an incoherent mess.

BLUE CHRISTMAS

Release Date: November 23, 1978
Alternate Titles: *Blood Type: Blue; The Blue Stigma; UFO Blue Christmas*

DIRECTED BY: Kihachi Okamoto
SCREENPLAY BY: So Kuramoto MUSIC BY: Masaru Sato CAST: Hiroshi Katsuno (Oki), Keiko Takeshita (Saeko Nishida), Nakadai Tatsuya (Minami Ichiya), Eiji Okada (Dr. Hyodo), Kaoru Yachigusa (Mrs. Hyodo), Kuni Tanaka (Kazuo Nishida)

Widescreen, Eastmancolor, 133 Minutes

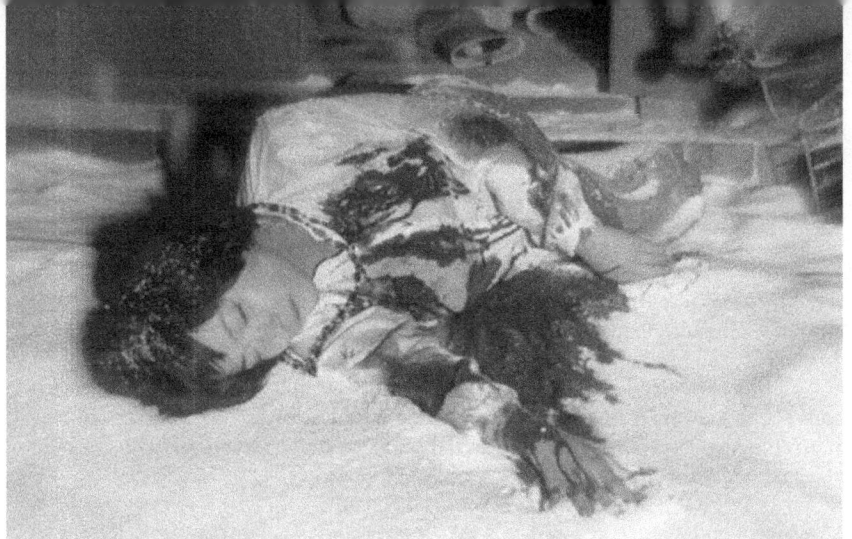

Saeko (Keiko Takeshita) meets her end in **BLUE CHRISTMAS**. © 1978 TOHO CO., LTD.

SYNOPSIS During the Christmas season of 1977, the earth witnesses a rash of strange U.F.O. sightings. The blood of those who witnesses these U.F.O.s turns blue in color. A prominent researcher of the phenomena, Dr. Hyodo, goes missing in America. Journalist Minami goes to New York where he tracks down Dr. Hyodo. However, he is advised to let the matter of what is happening to the blue-blooded people drop before Dr. Hyodo is escorted away by mysterious men. Upon returning to Japan, Minami is transferred to Paris. Meanwhile, Special Forces operative Oki keeps tabs upon the blue bloods as the government decides what to do about them as the year progresses. Oki falls in love with a lonely woman named Saeko, whom he only later discovers has blue blood. He is soon given orders from the government that on Christmas Day, 1978, all blue bloods are to be executed. Oki kills Saeko, and then turns his gun in anger at his fellow soldiers who proceed to murder him in cold blood. Elsewhere around the world, everyone with blue blood is murdered in a horrendous genocide.

OVERVIEW: By now, most western tokusatsu fans have heard of all of Toho's many sci-fi and fantasy films, but there are a few that occasionally slip through the cracks. One such film that many western fans have never heard of is Toho's 1978 *Close Encounters of the Third Kind*-inspired *Blue Christmas*.

Blue Christmas not only features no special effects scenes despite its premise, but was also one of the few Toho sci-fi films not produced by Tomoyuki Tanaka, who had recently transitioned to the President of Toho Co., Ltd. That said, Tanaka was still responsible for the production. In 1977, he saw So Kuramoto's original story in *Kinema Junpo* and decided to make a movie out of it. Like the film, the story centered on government/media paranoia over people recently abducted by U.F.O.s.

Tanaka wisely chose a director who had an affinity for U.F.O.s, the famed Kihachi Okamoto (*Sword of Doom, Kill!*), to helm the film adaptation. Okamoto was wise enough to begin filming some exterior location shots during the Christmas season of 1977 since the film obviously could not shoot the larger exterior Christmas scenes during the holiday season of 1978 when it would be released. Apparently, there was some friction between writer Kuramoto and Okamoto because Kuramoto insisted his script be 100% unaltered and adapted as it was written. The main problem with Kuramoto's script was that it was "as thick as a phonebook" so presumably some scenes were cut in order to bring it to a still lengthy runtime of 133 minutes. There was at least one scene that was cut involving the White House in America. An outtake from this scene appears in the movie's trailer with an actor playing the U.S. president, who otherwise does not appear in the film, remarking "Must I do what Hitler did?" Another deleted scene showed the special forces attacking a large group of people in Hokkaido and supposedly stills of this scene existed in an issue of *Kinema Junpo*.

Though clearly inspired by 1977's *Close Encounters of the Third Kind*, this film is far more downbeat, and may be the most depressing movie Toho's ever made. The story plays out over the span of one year, starting with the aftermath of Christmas 1977 where people across the world report not only having seen U.F.O.s, but their blood changing color to blue. A famous Japanese pop singer commits suicide when she discovers that her blood has turned blue.

Actually, we never do learn why the U.F.O. viewers' blood has turned blue or what the world's governments' problems with them are. Nor do we ever see the U.F.O.s, but truth be told, we don't need to and they would add nothing to the story. Ironically, not seeing the U.F.O.s almost adds to the real world feel of the story. After all, how many things do we hear about reported in the news which we do not ever see personally? Although some may find this tactic disappointing, it really only enhances the film and its pervading sense of paranoia.

The film's real merits exist in its mood and how the mystery is unraveled. This is aided along by the music by Masaru Sato, which is creepy and atmospheric. A particularly good example of this is a scene where headlines about the U.F.O.s play over Christmas music. This otherwise excellent 70s conspiracy thriller is unfortunately marred by a segment wherein Minami travels to New York in search of Dr. Hyodo. While the Caucasian actors in these scenes are actually quite good compared to similar gaijin actors in other films, here it is the situation itself that is ludicrous as Minami wanders New York asking random passersby—even bums—if they have seen the doctor! Eventually, Minami does find the doctor, and in a scene made popular in many of the era's conspiracy thrillers, Dr. Hyodo is escorted away by mysterious black clad men in a cemetery.

The film shifts its lead characters in the last act from Minami to military man Oki. It's debatable whether or not this really detracts from the film, but it is somewhat strange the two character's portions of the film aren't better intercut. In fact, Minami's last significant moment is seeing a lobotomized Dr. Hyodo in Paris, a rather large coincidence all things considered (though a rather disturbing end to the mystery). The love story between Oki and Saeko manages to be quite intriguing. The audience and Oki only discover that Saeko is one of the blue bloods after they have made love for the first time and at the film's end, Oki and a regiment of soldiers are ordered to gun down all of them.

To make matters more tragic, Saeko tells Oki how she was supposed to have a special date with her boyfriend on Christmas night in her home several years ago but he stood her up. Saeko asks Oki then if he will come to her home on Christmas night. In a heartbreaking turn, Oki is soon thereafter informed that on Christmas night, all blue bloods will be ambushed in their homes and executed. From there the tension mounts, as we wonder just what choice

Oki will make—and unfortunately, this ending is spoiled in the film's trailer. Still, the scenes leading up to the inevitable are well done, as they cut back and forth between an excited Saeko decorating her home for the night and Oki preparing for his mission.

Shockingly, Oki chooses not to save Saeko and is instead the very man to gun her down in her home. Naturally, Saeko merely thinks he's keeping his promise to spend Christmas night with her as he walks in the door. They lock eyes and he shoots her. Oki then goes outside to turn his gun on his fellow soldiers who gun him down. If this is a spur of the moment reaction or if Oki had planned this as a double-suicide all along, is unknown to the viewer. From there, we witness a montage of all the blue-blooded people of the world being graphically gunned down to Christmas music. The film then ends with a shot of Saeko's blue blood running down through the snow until it mixes in with Oki's red, implying that the color of people's blood never really mattered in the end.

Though it's frustrating the film ends with the viewer not knowing the governments' motives for committing a worldwide genocide, questions are always more alluring than answers. Though not terribly well remembered today, among this film's fans were Hideaki Anno who integrated elements of the film into his *Evangelion* series.

BLUE CHRISTMAS © 1978 TOHO CO., LTD.

VIRUS

Release Date: June 28, 1980
Japanese Title: *Resurrection Day*

DIRECTED BY: Kinji Fukasaku SPECIAL EFFECTS BY: Ichirô Higa & Warren Keillor SCREENPLAY BY: Koji Takada, Gregory Knapp, Kinji Fukasaku & Sakyo Komatsu (novel) MUSIC BY: Kentaro Haneda & Teo Macero CAST: Masao Kusakari (Dr. Shûzô Yoshizumi), Tsunehiko Watase (Yasuo Tatsuno), George Kennedy (Admiral Conway), Bo Svenson (Major Carter), Olivia Hussey (Marit), Shinichi "Sonny" Chiba (Dr. Yamauchi), Kensaku Morita (Takashi Mazawa), Toshiyuki Nagashima (Matsuo Akimasa), Glenn Ford (President Richardson), Robert Vaughn (Senator Barkley), Chuck Connors (Captain McCloud), Henry Silva (General Garland), George Touliatos (Colonel Rankin), Edward James Olmos (Captain Lopez)

Widescreen, Eastmancolor,
156 Minutes

THE LOST FILMS FANZINE PRESENTS MOVIE MILESTONES #3

Many of VIRUS's major stars including George Kennedy, Edward James Olmos, Masao Kusakari, and Bo Svenson. VIRUS © 1980 KADOKAWA/TOHO CO., LTD.

SYNOPSIS In the early months of 1982, a deadly virus is accidentally unleashed upon the world. An epidemic slowly begins to spread. At the White House, President Richardson argues with Colonel Rankin about whether or not to activate their nuclear defenses, called the ARS, against the Russians. Richardson commands him not to but eventually, he succumbs to the virus and Garland heads into a bunker to activate the ARS. By autumn, nearly all of humanity is dead. Under the leadership of Admiral Conway, only 863 people survive at an outpost in Antarctica where it is too cold for the virus to survive. Over time, mankind becomes resigned to their fate at the South Pole until earthquake expert Dr. Yoshizumi makes a startling discovery: an impending earthquake will soon set off the ARS in Washington. When it does, their outpost will be destroyed. Yoshizumi heads out in the British submarine *Nereid* with Major Carter to stop the launch. They are too late and the earthquake occurs, Carter is killed, and the missiles launch. The outpost in Antarctica is evacuated just in time and humanity survives. Yoshizumi then treks on foot across two continents to reunite with the survivors, among them his love Marit.

OVERVIEW Before sinking Japan in his 1973 novel, author Sakyo Komatsu first decided to decimate the entire earth with a deadly virus in his novel *Resurrection Day* in 1964. Long before the film eventually came to the big screen in 1980, Toho considered adapting the book in 1965. However, Toho quickly decided that the film was outside of their usual scope, as it would need international stars and locations.

And so Komatsu had his story translated into English and shopped it around the U.S. There it eventually caught the eye of 20th Century Fox in the late 1960s. Trouble arose in 1969 when

Michael Crichton's novel *The Andromeda Strain* became a bestseller and was optioned for the big screen. You see, the problem was that in Komatsu's novel the virus came from outer space. Therefore it was now considered too similar to *Andromeda Strain* to adapt. And so the film was dropped by 20th century Fox.

The story was optioned again by the giant publishing magnate turned aspiring movie mogul Haruki Kadokawa in 1974. However, it would take the movie over five years to begin filming (and the idea of the virus being from outer space was dropped so as to avoid comparisons to *Andromeda Strain*). Kadokawa had high hopes for the film, and tried to lure popular directors such as John Frankenheimer and Giorgi Pan Costmas to the project, but they weren't interested. As such, Kadokawa had to settle for Kinji Fukasaku, who typically directed Yakuza movies (plus Toei's recent big budget *Message from Space* in 1978). Though *Submersion of Japan's* Shiro Moritani was also considered, for whatever reason he was passed over (either that, or he was unavailable, it's tough to say).

Fukusaku went location scouting in the winter of 1978 for 90 days. When filming finally began, the shoot lasted for over 200 days all across the world. The crew traveled to locales as diverse as the Machu Picchu ruins in South America to Antarctica itself. A real submarine from the Chilean Navy was even utilized, so no expense was spared, and that included the actors.

Perhaps tired of the poor performances of many gaijin actors in tokusatsu films, Kadokawa shelled out big bucks for American stars—not superstars, mind you—but stars nonetheless recognizable across the world. Of the more prominent names, George Kennedy gets the most screentime, mainly because his character is one of the few to survive. The other two big stars, Glenn Ford and Robert Vaughn as the president and a senator respectively, put in excellent performances, but their characters die within the first act of the film.

Despite its lackluster reputation brought about by its severely truncated U.S. version, the original version of *Virus* is a great disaster film—something in between *Submersion of Japan* and *Prophecies of Nostradamus (Catastrophe 1999)*. By comparison, *Submersion of Japan* focused on a single cataclysmic event (the sinking of Japan) and *Prophecies of Nostradamus* offered a look at every conceivable disaster possible (from zombies to nuclear war to extreme climate change). In *Virus*, one disaster feeds the next, and all of them are brought about by mankind. Human error unleashes the virus, which decimates the population. A rogue general in Washington brings a nuclear missile defense system online and an earthquake just happens to launch the nukes. The storyline goes from a virus to an earthquake to an all-out nuclear holocaust.

Though *Virus* has the huge star-studded ensemble typical of disaster films, the heart and soul of the film is *ESPY* star Masao Kusakari as Dr. Shuzo Yoshizumi. Shuzo notably forms a unique bond with Bo Svenson's Major Carter character. It is this duo who tries and fails to prevent the launching of the nukes in Washington. Carter's death in the arms of Shuzo is a touching scene, edited down in the truncated U.S. cut. In the film's lengthy epilogue, Shuzo must literally traverse two continents on foot to return to his fellow survivors. His reunion with them at the end of the film is somehow uplifting and downbeat at the same time. Having endured so much tragedy, Shuzo remarks that even in the post-apocalyptic wasteland, life is beautiful when reunited with loved ones.

Though it has a few clunky moments here and there, *Virus* is on par with many U.S. disaster films. If not for a large number of scenes set in Japan, one might even mistake the movie for a Hollywood production. Haruki Kadokawa had succeeded in making a "panic movie" that could appeal to international audiences. Sadly, though the film did turn a profit in Japan, Virus was too late to the party to ride the coattails of U.S. disaster movies abroad. A "work-in-progress" cut of the movie screened at the Cannes Film Festival in May of 1980 failed to impress. Virus, the most lavish Japanese production of all time with big American stars to boot, would fail to see a theatrical release stateside. Instead, it was cut down to 108 minutes and sent directly to cable (though there also existed a 93-minute version likely made for general broadcast standards to cut out disturbing scenes too intense for TV). That version—which forgoes the epilogue, leaving Yoshizumi's fate uncertain—is an incomprehensible mess and should be avoided... like a virus.

Virus may not be a masterpiece like *Submersion of Japan*, but it's a great disaster film in its own right and much better than the two Komatsu films to follow (*Sayonara Jupiter* and *Tokyo Blackout*). It is also reportedly Komatsu's favorite adaptation of one of his novels.

THE BOOK VS. THE MOVIE The VIRUS film adaptation is a rare case of the movie being better than the book. Fundamentally the outline of the two are the same aside from two major details: additional characters and the origin of the virus. As stated earlier, the virus's origin was actually from outer space (the MM in MM88 even means Martian Murderer). This detail doesn't impact the story structure much, but it's certainly interesting. The main effect it does have comes down to the ending. In the book, Neutron Missiles launched by Russia's ARS system mutate the space virus into a new form that is less harmful to humans, hence their survival.

The end portion in Washington D.C. is fairly different. In the film, Carter dies from wounds received during the quake, but in the book it's due to a venomous snakebite! While the book doesn't explain how snakes survived the plague while many other animals didn't, Carter accidentally walks into a nest of vipers and is bitten. Later, after he and Yoshizumi fail to disengage ARS, Carter is dying from the venom. When Yoshizumi's back is turned, Carter shoots himself, committing suicide.

The novel had next to no female characters of significance aside from Noriko, who is a reporter rather than a nurse as in the movie (nor was there a pregnancy subplot for Noriko and Yoshizumi as in the film). Merit, Yoshizumi's love interest in Antarctica, isn't in the book at all and was likely created to give the movie a proper female lead. This naturally lessens the story's final scene where Yoshizumi reunites with his group. In the movie he gets a happy reunion with Merit. In the book, Yoshizumi has no one of significance to return to. On top of that, he's also completely insane, while in the film he's just worn down.

SYNOPSIS Young and upcoming geologist Yoichi Kawazu predicts that an earthquake will strike Tokyo within thirty days due to recent activity at Mt. Mihara. Kawazu's colleagues at the Earthquake Prevention Center are outraged at his bold claims and suppress his theory. Kawazu shares the news with Tomiko, a lab assistant he is having an affair with, who in turn shares it with her reporter friend Hashizume. When Kawazu's wife Yuko demands a divorce, she also requests to meet Tomiko face to face. On the way to see Tomiko via subway, Kawazu and his wife are trapped underground when the earthquake hits and devastates Tokyo. Because they ignored Kawazu's warnings, the Japanese government is absolutely helpless to do anything to help people in Tokyo. Kawazu sacrifices himself to save his wife and other survivors by blowing out a hole keeping rushing water in that would soon drown everyone, while Hashizume rescues Tomiko in a skyscraper amidst a blazing Tokyo.

DEATHQUAKE

Release Date: August 30, 1980
Alternate Titles: *Earthquake Archipelago* (Japan) *Magnitude 7.9* (unknown) *Megaforce 7.9* (UK) *Earthquake '81* (Spain)

DIRECTED BY: Kenjiro Omori SPECIAL EFFECTS BY: Teruyoshi Nakano SCREENPLAY BY: Kaneto Shindo MUSIC BY: Toshiaki Tsushima CAST: Hiroshi Katsuno (Yoichi Kawazu), Kayo Matsuo (Yuko Kawazu), Toshiyuki Nagashima (Masayuki Hashizume), Yumi Takigawa (Tomiko Ashida), Shuji Otaki (Professor Marumo), Shin Saburi (Prime Minister)

Widescreen, Color, 126 Minutes

SPECIAL PREVIEW!!!

THE LOST FILMS FANZINE is pleased to present a special preview of author Jules Carrozza's SF: THE JAPANESE SCIENCE FICTION FILM ENCYCLOPEDIA via the book's entry for DEATHQUAKE! (Note: the following text is copyright Jules L. Carrozza and Orochi Books. The images appear here for the sake of illustrating the article and are copyright Toho Co., Ltd DEATHQUAKE 1980 and do not appear in the book.)

Toho would revive its disaster film cycle with 1980's *Deathquake*. They had, earlier in the year, produced a TV movie called *Tokyo Earthquake Magnitude 8.1*. The cast led by Sonny Chiba, ratings were through the roof. So a lavish-budgeted theatrical film was green-lit. *Deathquake's* tagline goes "I knew it would come someday, I just hoped it wouldn't be today". Like *Submersion of Japan*, it dwells on the existential horror eternally facing the people of Tokyo. That is, the possibility of another horrific earthquake on par with the great Kanto quake of 1923. The fact is, a severe Tokyo earthquake with an epicenter near the Kanto region is overdue. Such a quake would likely dwarf the devastation wrought by the 3/11 earthquake and tsunami in 2011. *Deathquake* proposes this, served with a mix of pathos and Irwin Allen-like spectacle.

Deathquake features an engaging script by Kaneto Shindo, director of *The Island*, *Onibaba* and *Kuroneko*. It features seismologist Dr. Kawazu (Hiroshi Katsuno), who realizes that the next Kanto earthquake is only a month away. Kawazu puts his career on the line as he desperately tries to convince his colleagues. Nobody listens of course, with the exception of his mistress (Yumi Takigawa who just caught the lethal MM88 in *Virus* that same summer). An intrepid young reporter (Toshiyuki Nagashima, who later appeared in *Gamera 2*) is also intrigued. The Prime Minister (Kentaro Kaji) is far more interested in improving his golf swing than listening to Kawazu's apocalyptic predictions. The trope of a rebellious outlier fighting to convince Japan's bureaucratic establishment the sky is falling foreshadows *Shin Godzilla*. Of course, Kawazu is right and a monstrous 7.9 magnitude quake turns Tokyo into a burning hellscape. In the end, Kawazu is trapped in a flooding underground subway with his soon to be ex-wife (*Lone Wolf and Cub's* Kayo Matsuo). He has to make a sacrifice that seems almost kamikaze-like to Western viewers.

Deathquake, until that point a family drama, springs to life once the tremors start. Teruyoshi "Bomber" Nakano's unit takes center stage and the film is possibly Nakano's fiery masterwork. The miniature work is top tier and the pyrotechnics so plentiful you can almost feel the heat. Nakano's work on *Deathquake* is like an intricate dance with burning gasoline and model buildings, barraging the viewer with one stunning tokusatsu conflagration after another. Director Kenjiro Omori's unit also produces footage that is suspensefully helmed. Tilting, rotating sets are used inventively to simulate tremors. The two units' footage is almost seamlessly integrated and the production values are stunning. As with much of Toho's output from this period, *Deathquake* is quite criminally underrated.

J.L. CARROZZA
JLカーローザー

SF:
THE JAPANESE SCIENCE FICTION FILM ENCYCLOPEDIA
日本のSF映画百科事典

Informed by its disaster-prone history, Japan's science fiction cinema is distinctive. SF covers a wide variety of these films across six decades; from the aftermath of Hiroshima to the COVID-19 pandemic. Included are monster classics like GODZILLA, MOTHRA and GAMERA, apocalyptic epics like SUBMERSION OF JAPAN and VIRUS and offbeat works like THE FACE OF ANOTHER and TETSUO: THE IRON MAN. This book features eye-opening analyses of dozens of Japanese sci-fi films along with insightful capsule reviews for many more. SF will appeal to casual fans looking to learn more and obsessed initiates alike.

This book also contains informative articles by Carrozza and others including Patrick Galvan, Kevin Derendorf and John LeMay. Read insider information on the filmmakers who brought the films to life. Find out about amazing luminaries of the genre. Ishiro Honda. Eiji Tsuburaya. Kobo Abe. Sakyo Komatsu. Kinji Fukasaku. Hideaki Anno and many others. Discover the artisan techniques of the old school Japanese film industry. Learn about everything from home video releases to English dubbing to the genre's influence on other East Asian countries.

SF: THE JAPANESE SCIENCE FICTION FILM ENCYLOPEDIA promises to enlighten you on an underappreciated genre from a culture that has tasted the apocalypse and lived to tell about it.

SAYONARA JUPITER

Alternate Titles: *Sayonara Jupiter* (Japan) *Goodbye, Jupiter, Goodbye* (Spain) *Asalenian Vultures of Space* (Greece) *Operation Jupiter* (Germany)
Release Date: March 17, 1984

DIRECTED BY: Sakyo Komatsu & Koji Hashimoto SPECIAL EFFECTS BY: Koichi Kawakita SCREENPLAY BY: Sakyo Komatsu MUSIC BY: Kentaro Haneda CAST: Tomokazu Miura (Dr. Eiji Honda), Diane D'Angely (Maria Basehart), Miyuki Ono (Anita), Rachel Huggert (Dr. Millicent Wilem), Marc Panthona (Carlos), William Tapier (Webb), Akihiko Hirata (Dr. Ryutaro Inoue), Masumi Okada (Dr. Mohammed Mansur), Ron Irwin (Captain Kinn), Kim Bass (Booker), Paul Tagawa (Peter)

Widescreen, Color, 127 Minutes

SYNOPSIS In 2125 A.D., mankind has colonized both the moon as well as Mars. To counter the ever-increasing population, the Jupiter Solarization Program—a plan to ignite Jupiter into a second sun—is born. In charge of the project is scientist Eiji Honda, who encounters trouble when a sect of the Jupiter Church—a group of environmentalists of sorts—sabotages the space station orbiting Jupiter. Things get worse when Eiji learns one of the saboteurs is his ex-girlfriend Maria and also that a black hole is headed towards the solar system and it will eventually engulf the earth on its current path. Eiji concocts a plan to move Jupiter into the path of the black hole, in hopes that Jupiter can knock the black hole onto another trajectory out of the Milky Way. When the plan goes into effect and the final countdown begins, the Jupiter Church again manages to sabotage the mission. In the process, Eiji shoots and mortally wounds Maria, who then tells Eiji where to find the bombs that the eco-terrorists have hidden around the space station. In the nick of time, Eiji manages to eject all the bombs but one, and is injured in the explosion. He and Maria lay dying together as the ship crashes into Jupiter. The planet collides with the black hole and as it is engulfed, manages to divert the black hole onto a path out of the solar system.

OVERVIEW: The development of Toho's final Showa era disaster film is a curious one which, as always, seems to have conflicting accounts about its development. The most common account states that the film's genesis lies in 1977 when Tomoyuki Tanaka saw *Star Wars* at a screening in Hawaii. Tanaka returned to Japan and requested hit-maker Sakyo Komatsu to write a *Star Wars*-inspired film. Komatsu ignored the *Star Wars*

THE LOST FILMS FANZINE PRESENTS MOVIE MILESTONES #3

Tomokazu Miura as Eiji Honda and Diane D'Angely as Maria. BYE, BYE JUPITER © 1984 TOHO CO., LTD.

idea, and assembled a team of writers that began meeting in September of that year. From these meetings supposedly sprang something called *Battle of the Galactic Empire*. An alternative to this tale says that Komatsu was already thinking about a space-based sci-fi film in 1976 before Tanaka ever saw *Star Wars*. This comes from *Toho Special Effects Movie Complete Works* and the book states it was planned to be an animated TV movie or series.

Whatever the case, Komatsu took too long for Tanaka's liking and he commissioned an outer space remake of *Atragon* instead from Shuichi Nagahara. This film became the rather rushed *The War in Space*, and Komatsu continued working on his idea separately. In fact, Komatsu hoped to take it to Hollywood rather than Toho and made sure that his second draft contained space battles similar to *Star Wars*. However, Komatsu eventually realized he didn't wish to compete with *Star Wars*, and so cut the space battles and created a more introspective story.

Komatsu took his idea to Hollywood, pitching it to as many studio executives as he could. One of the execs was none other than Alan Ladd, who had greenlit *Star Wars* but did not greenlight Komatsu's idea. However, not all the studios rejected Komatsu's idea. One agreed to produce the film but Komatsu would not be allowed to contribute from that point forward and so the author refused. Komatsu, who had hoped his film could star Orson Wells, instead went back to Japan and turned the story into a novel serialized in May of 1980 in *Weekly Sankei*. In 1981, Komatsu even created his own small film company, IO, to get the movie off of the ground. From his novel, he not only created the third draft but also storyboards and a possible shooting schedule. Komatsu even hired designers for concept drawings and physical models of which he shot test footage. Sadly, Toho told him his third draft script was unfilmable on a technical level. This didn't mean Toho rejected the script, however, and in June of 1982, Toho made their plans official to make Komatsu's film on a more limited scale.

In choosing a director, originally *Submersion of Japan's* Shiro Moritani was the main contender. However, Moritani became ill soon after he was chosen and so his second unit director on that film, Koji Hashimoto, was chosen instead. *House* director Nobuhiko Obayashi was also considered as director at one point but was rejected due to being "too difficult to control." Komatsu handed over the script to director Koji Hashimoto who drastically cut the script, combining characters and compressing the story in order to shorten the lengthy running time. The final version of the story was completed in March of 1983.

The original ¥1.8 billion budget was slashed significantly to only 1/3rd of the original budget but was still considerably large for the time. Filming began in April of 1983 with Koichi Kawakita in charge of the special effects. Hashimoto began shooting with actors that May. In a rare instance of an author directing the motion picture adaptation of their book, Komatsu was allowed to co-direct with Hashimoto. Actually, Komatsu even helped to set-up miniatures in some shots! In terms of effects, it was a groundbreaking production and involved the first use of computer generated imagery in a Japanese film as well as motion camera control.

BYE, BYE JUPITER © 1984 TOHO CO., LTD.

The production had finished shooting in October of 1983 and then began the long post-production process. In the end, the film had cost ¥600,000,000, but that cost ballooned to around ¥1 billion by the time of post-production and promotion costs. Toho had faith in the film due to the success of Komatsu's past adaptations. However, due to the huge budget, the film's grosses were not enough to make the massive production worthwhile and was considered a failure at the box office.

Critically the film was a dud, with Komatsu's own fans sometimes hitting it hardest. One wrote that, "Komatsu revealed that his talent is limited to novels." Even Koichi Kawakita said in an interview that he preferred the edited-down version of the film that aired on Japanese TV that cut out all sequences on earth. Kawakita said to David Milner of the TV version that, "I prefer the edited version. I share Sakyo Komatsu's concerns about the environment, but I feel that the scenes which take place at the Jupiter Foundation are not necessary."

Despite its big budget appeal, *Sayonara Jupiter* never secured a U.S. release of any sort until it was issued to a special edition DVD by Discotek in 2007. Toho's international version (*Bye-Bye Jupiter*) did manage to make it to several other countries, though.

THE RETURN OF GODZILLA

Release Date: December 15, 1984
Alternate Titles: *Godzilla* (Japan) *Godzilla 1985* (U.S.) *Godzilla: The Return of the Monsters* (Germany) *Godzilla Returns* (Norway)

DIRECTED BY: Koji Hashimoto SPECIAL EFFECTS BY: Teruyoshi Nakano SCREENPLAY BY: Shuichi Nagahara MUSIC BY: Reijiro Koroku CAST: Keiju Kobayashi (Prime Minister Seiki Mitamura), Ken Tanaka (Goro Maki), Yasuko Sawaguchi (Naoko Okumura), Yosuke Natsuki (Professor Hayashida), Shin Takuma (Hiroshi Okumura) SUIT PERFORMERS: Kenpachiro Satsuma (Godzilla)

Widescreen, Color, 103 Minutes

SYNOPSIS Okumura, the lone survivor of an encounter with something that is determined to be Godzilla, is rescued at sea by reporter Goro Maki. The two team with Okumura's mentor, Professor Hayashida, and Okumura's sister Naoko to investigate Godzilla when he comes ashore in Japan to draw energy from a nuclear power plant. Hayashida notices the way the monster follows a flock of birds and concludes that Godzilla can be lured with the same frequency wave emitted by birds when they fly. The monster lands in Tokyo where he engages the new weapon Super X and is poisoned by its cadmium missiles. When a nuclear missile is accidentally launched by a Russian tanker in Tokyo Bay, the Americans send a missile to intercept it and the city is saved, but the resulting thermonuclear blast in the stratosphere revives Godzilla. Hayashida uses his wave device to lure Godzilla to Mt. Mihara on Oshima Island and manages to dump the monster inside the volcano.

OVERVIEW: Yes Virginia, *The Return of Godzilla* is actually a Panic Movie. Here's why. Unlike all of the other Godzilla movies to follow the 1954 original, in which Godzilla fought an opponent, this movie is squarely about Godzilla attacking Tokyo. Once Godzilla's existence is confirmed early in the film, characters spend most of their time preparing for and dreading his arrival. They even know how to defeat the monster well before the third act, making Godzilla, in a sense, not unlike a passing storm, earthquake, or other force of nature (which was more or less the film's aim). This atmosphere is not surprising considering the director, Koji Hashimoto, also helmed Toho's big-budget space disaster *Sayonara Jupiter*. Adding to the disaster feel is the significant cold war subplot where the Russians accidentally launch a nuclear warhead at Tokyo (that alone could have probably served as the basis for its own Panic Movie.) The erupting volcano that Godzilla falls into at the end also fits well into a Panic Movie (and Mt. Mihara had been featured earlier that decade in Toho's *Deathquake*.)

Reijiro Koroku's score reaches maximum effect, usually gloomy and downbeat—the only exceptions being the Super X theme and the Self Defense Force March and a few others. The man would've been a worthy successor to Akira Ifukube had he ever been asked to return. And for the first time in many years, Godzilla appears without an enemy monster to face (though he does engage in a rousing battle with the Super X—a sort of flying fortress). Not surprisingly, Godzilla's two main sequences, the destruction of the Ihama nuclear power plant and the raid on Tokyo, are the film's highlights. Notably, the monster appears only at night and sports a snarling visage that always looks intimidating. Overall, Godzilla's attack on Tokyo is one of the best city destruction sequences in kaiju eiga history. That said, contrary to popular opinion, Godzilla doesn't really "destroy" Tokyo. He mostly wanders through it, not unlike a tourist, and doesn't become overly destructive or aggressive until attacked by the military.

In terms of special effects Teruyoshi Nakano actually does so well with his higher budget effects that one would be hard pressed to believe the same man directed the effects for 1973's *Godzilla vs. Megalon*. In addition to traditional suitmation, the new film employed a much-ballyhooed 15-foot-tall Cybot Godzilla, though it was rarely used in the film itself and was more useful to the studio as a publicity tool for various press displays. It was also a good reason to proclaim that Godzilla wasn't "just a man in a suit" anymore, though it is the man in the suit, Kenpachiro Satsuma (formerly known as Kengo Nakayama) that gives the monster's best performance. The suit was intended for a much larger man, but when he bowed out Satsuma, previously Gigan and Hedorah, stepped into the role.

Toho's big-budget investment in rebooting Godzilla paid off much better than it had for the same year's *Sayonara Jupiter* and managed to sell 3.5 million tickets (¥1.7 billion) in Japan making it the second-highest grossing domestic film of 1984. However, as the film cost around $6 million to produce, $1 million to market and grossed around $7 million, Toho still made most of their profits off the tie-in merchandising, which itself was monstrous.

UNMADE FILES: GODZILLA: GOD'S ANGRY MESSENGER One of Toho's earlier, aborted attempts to revive Godzilla in 1979 was also patented after a Panic Movie, specifically PROPHECIES OF NOSTRADAMUS. It was inspired by CHARIOTS OF THE GODS and had Godzilla as a dinosaur engineered by aliens in the past that fulfills the Biblical prophecy of Armageddon!

THE RETURN OF GODZILLA © 1984 TOHO CO. LTD.

THE LOST FILMS FANZINE PRESENTS MOVIE MILESTONES #3

TOKYO BLACKOUT

Release Date: January 17, 1987
Japanese Title: *Disappearance of the Capital*

DIRECTED BY: Toshio Masuda SPECIAL EFFECTS BY: Teruyoshi Nakano SCREENPLAY BY: Toshio Masuda, Hiroyasu Yamamura & Sakyo Komatsu (novel) MUSIC BY: Maurice Jarre CAST: Tsunehiko Watase (Tatsuya Asakura), Yuko Natori (Mariko Koide), Shinji Yamashita (Yosuke Tamiya), Yoko Ishino (Mieko Matsunaga), Shuji Otaki (Gonzo Otawara), Isao Natsuyagi (Eiji Sakuma), Tetsuro Tamba (Delegate Nakata), Midori Ebina (Keiko Yasuhara), Eimei Esumi (Takeda), Haruko Kato (Umeko Koide), Ittoku Kishibe (Yasuhara)

Widescreen, Color, 120 Minutes

SYNOPSIS When Tokyo is unexpectedly enveloped by a mysterious electromagnetic cloud, the world is stunned. All communication is lost within the capital and the U.S. pressures Japan to form a new government. In the middle of the investigation are reporters Asakura and Mariko who desperately want to get back inside the city so Mariko can see her daughter. A scientific means of breaching the cloud is developed through a new machine. Two of the machines are mounted to military vehicles but when they attempt to breach the cloud, it begins to draw them in, so they retreat. A brave general drives one of the trucks back into the cloud and seems to cause some effect. Asakura boards the second truck and barrels into the cloud. Finally, it begins to open and dissipate. Asakura and Mariko walk into Tokyo for the first time, hoping to find survivors. When they find a lost dog, the cloud lifts entirely....

OVERVIEW: After *Submersion of Japan* (1973) and *ESPY* (1974) became back-to-back big hits, the stories' creator, Sakyo Komatsu, became a hot property in the Japan film industry. The year 1980 saw his novel *Resurrection Day* adapted as the most expensive Japanese film up to that time. His next work, *Sayonara Jupiter* (1984), was a bit too expensive to make much of a profit. So Komatsu's next adapted work, *Capital City Disappears*, would end up being something of a gamble. The story was initially serialized from December of 1983 to December of 1984 in the *Hokkaido Shimbun*, *Chunichi Shimbun*, and the *West Japan Newspaper*. The story was well received and even won the 6th Japan SF Award. Naturally, Komatsu's story was optioned for film a few years later. Rather than Toho alone, it would be a co-production between Toho and Tokuma Shoten (which had purchased

The alien cloud over Tokyo. TOKYO BLACKOUT © 1987 KADOKAWA/DAIE/TOHO CO., LTD.

Daiei in the late 70s) along with Kansai Telecasting (KTV).

Even though it's set in the late 1980s, *Tokyo Blackout* still has all the usual tropes of a Japanese science fiction film of the 1950s and 60s. As usual, a pair of reporters anchor the film and are surrounded by various scientists and military men. The film's problem is also solved by the creation of a scientifically advanced mech. The ending is as well done as it can be, with a good deal of suspense being generated by the machines trying to breach the wall. After two failed attempts, it is finally the film's hero Asakura who breaches the wall. Asakura and the female lead, Mariko (who has a daughter trapped in the city) tepidly enter the city for the first time since the cloud appeared. At first, it seems that the film is going to end on a depressing note much like 2007's *The Mist*. But, Asakura finds a puppy amongst the wreckage. If a puppy can survive, perhaps so too did the residents of Tokyo. The couple walk into the dissipating cloud hopefully and the film comes to a close revealing that Tokyo still stands, and only the outskirts were charred by the cloud.

The film more or less follows the novel for the first half, but begins to deviate in the second half which is more proactive than the book regarding the rescue of those stuck inside Tokyo. In the book, things more or less resolve themselves, with the cloud mysteriously dissipating after a few months. The film, naturally requiring a sense of urgency for the audience, implies that manmade technology plays a role in getting the cloud to dissipate—or retreat as it is said to be an alien device of some sort. Like *Blue Christmas*, no aliens are ever seen and nor are their mysterious motives ever revealed.

Where the novel is different concerns the story's timetable. The movie takes place over a relatively short period of time, whereas in the book the cloud lingers over Tokyo for around four months before disappearing. The book

Some classic Japanese mech used to confront the cloud. TOKYO BLACKOUT © 1987 KADOKAWA/DAIEI/TOHO CO., LTD.

is also much more political, with the U.S. pressuring Japan to set up a new government being one of the focal points. A Soviet fleet also approaches Japan to investigate when an earthquake occurs and a tsunami hits. Apparently, Komatsu also envisioned the book ending with the cloud survivors developing enhanced intelligence and abilities but the idea was scrapped in favor of a more tidy end.

The book was also very similar to the 1964 story *Object O* where a ring-like object envelops Osaka which Komatsu also had a hand in writing. In *Tokyo Blackout*, there is even a scene where the cloud is referred to as Object O. The film's screenplay was written by director Toshio Masuda and Hiroyasu Yamamura, who had written many scripts for Tsuburaya Production's TV series like *Mirrorman*, *Ultraseven*, and *Dinosaur War Izenborg*. One of Yamamura's few motion picture credits included helping Jun Fukuda with the script for 1974's *Godzilla vs. Mechagodzilla*. As for Toshio Masuda, he was the director of 1974's controversial *Prophecies of Nostradamus*. Reuniting with Masuda was Toho's main special effects director Teruyoshi Nakano, who handled the effects work. This would be one of Nakano's last films, and he would retire (though, some feel he was pushed out by Toho in favor of the younger Koichi Kawakita) after the release of that same year's *Princess from the Moon*.

As for Nakano's work on this film it is naturally mostly devoted to the strange cloud itself. The cloud appears early in the film, enveloping Tokyo in a dark storm pulsing with lightning. A large aircraft carrier is destroyed when it tries to breach the cloud, so fans of miniature destruction don't have to wait too long to get their fix. Compared to the tidal waves, earthquakes, and other assorted natural or nuclear disasters from previous Japanese disaster films, a giant cloud can't offer much by comparison. But what it lacks for in destructive capability, it makes up for in mystery. That being said, there are a few instances of lightning causing some miniature

THE LOST FILMS FANZINE PRESENTS MOVIE MILESTONES #3

The stars of TOKYO BLACKOUT: Tsunehiko Watase & Yuko Natori. TOKYO BLACKOUT © 1987 KADOKAWA/DAIEI/TOHO CO., LTD.

destruction and Nakano does get to blow up a few buildings and oil tanks—though it really isn't much compared to his previous works.

The effects highlight of the film may well be when a U.S. air force plane flies over the cloud trying to breach it from above. Instead, the cloud attacks it with lightning and the plane begins to streak with green fire. Another great scene (which has a spooky *Ghostbusters* quality to it) concerns Asakura, Mariko, and the scientific team trying to enter the cloud from the ground. To their shock, nothing—not even bullets—can penetrate it. In all, about 100 tons of dry ice was used for the cloud effects. Teruyoshi Nakano even won a Japanese Academy Award for his effects work on the film.

If the film has one weak spot, it is ironically the score. The film's music composer was the famed French film composer Maurice Jarre who scored *Dr. Zhivago*, *Ghost*, and many other famous films. Unfortunately, one would be hard pressed to think that the composer of this film was the same man who composed classics like *Lawrence of Arabia*. Like many of Jarre's other scores, it is heavy on piano, but is very forgettable.

Earning ¥760,000,000, it's tough to decipher how well received the film was in Japan, but it certainly hasn't gone down as a classic like S*ubmersion of Japan*, nor is it remembered as a monumental flop like *Sayonara Jupiter*.

119

KOMATSU'S LEGACY

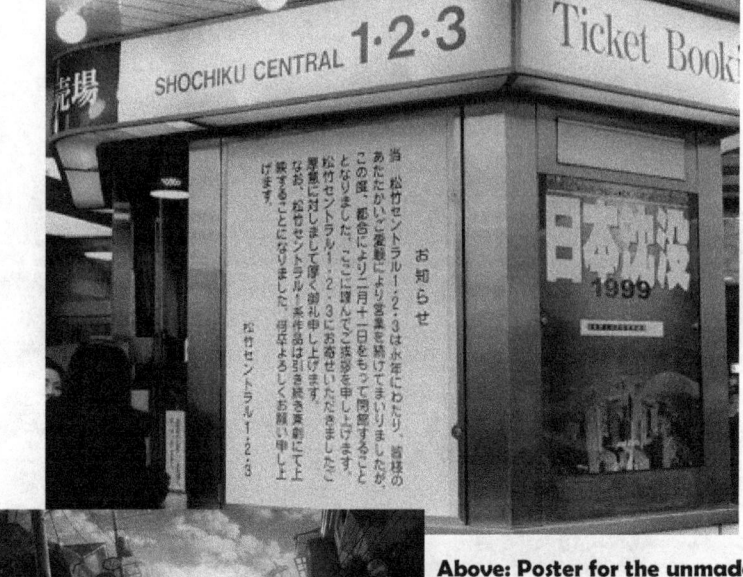

Above: Poster for the unmade 1999 JAPAN SINKS. Left: Ad for the JAPAN SINKS anime.

In some respects, *Tokyo Blackout* was Sakyo Komatsu's last major film adaptation or rather, the last one he was involved with. After this would be the 1989 TV series *Sakyo Komatsu's Anime Theater*. In 1998, there came rumblings of a remake of *Submersion of Japan*. That year, Shochiku announced plans to remake the film with Kazuki Omori directing and possibly writing (Omori was best known for the Heisei Godzilla films). The production was formally announced on September 30, 1998, at the Ginza Tokyo Hotel stating that the film would be a New Year's movie for 2000 released in December of 1999.

Things got serious enough that there was an advance trailer made that ran in theaters. Supposedly, the film was budgeted at ¥1.2 million with a hoped for gross of ¥3 billion. Omori, along with Sakyo Komatsu, was a victim of the Great Hanshin-Awaji Earthquake of 1995. Omori hoped to use the film to promote earthquake awareness amongst the younger generation. Shochiku hoped to utilize CGI for the film's special effects, though presumably miniatures would be used as well. However, Shochiku was not able to secure the funds to produce the film, and on March 5, 1999, Shochiku president Nobuyoshi Otani announced at a press conference that the production was cancelled.

Thankfully, seven years later a well-done remake in the form of *Japan Sinks* was completed. It was directed by Shinki Higuchi, who had become famous for his ground breaking effects on Daiei's 90s Gamera movies. The film was a sizeable hit that helped to laucnh his career.

As stated earlier, Komatsu passed away in 2011, but his works are still in print and are still being adapted to film. Most recently, in 2020, premiered the *Japan Sinks* anime on Netflix.

2006年、夏
すべて消える

草彅 剛　柴咲コウ

日本沈没

www.nc06.jp

THE LOST FILMS FANZINE PRESENTS MOVIE MILESTONES #3

THE BICEP BOOKS CATALOGUE

The following titles are available for purchase on Amazon.com, and are available to bookstores at a wholesale discount via Ingram Content Group (ISBNs of available editions listed for this purpose)

THE BIG BOOK OF JAPANESE GIANT MONSTER MOVIES SERIES

The third edition of the book that started it all! Reviews over 100 tokusatsu films between 1954 and 1988. All the Godzilla, Gamera, and Daimajin movies made during the Showa era are covered plus lesser known fare like *Invisible Man vs. The Human Fly* (1957) and *Conflagration* (1975). Softcover (380 pp/5.83" X 8.27") Suggested Retail: $19.99 ISBN: 978-1-7341546-4-1

This third edition reviews over 75 tokusatsu films between 1989 and 2019. All the Godzilla, Gamera, and Ultraman movies made during the Heisei era are covered plus independent films like *Reigo, King of the Sea Monsters* and *Attack of the Giant Teacher*! Softcover (260 pp/5.83" X 8.27") Suggested Retail: $19.99 ISBN: 978-1-7347816-4-9

Covering unproduced scripts like *Bride of Godzilla* (1955), partially shot movies like *Giant Horde Beast Nezura* (1963), and banned films like *Prophecies of Nostradamus* (1974), this second edition of the Rondo Award nominated book covers hundreds of lost productions. 470 pp. Softcover/ Hardcover (7" X 10") Suggested Retail: $24.99(sc)/$39.95(hc) ISBN: 978-1-7341546-0-3 (hc)

This sequel to *The Lost Films* covers the non-giant monster unmade movie scripts from Japan such as *Frankenstein vs. the Human Vapor* (1963), *After Japan Sinks* (1974-76), plus lost movies like *Fearful Attack of the Flying Saucers* (1956) and *Venus Flytrap* (1968). Hardcover (200 pp/5.83" X 8.27")/Softcover (216 pp/5.5" X 8.5") Suggested Retail: $9.99 (sc)/$24.99(hc) ISBN: 978-1-7341546-3-4 (hc)

This companion book to *The Lost Films* charts the development of all the prominent Japanese monster movies including discarded screenplays, story ideas, and deleted scenes. Also includes bios for writers like Shinichi Sekizawa, Niisan Takahashi and many others. Comprehensive script listing and appendices as well. Hardcover/ Softcover (370 pp./6" X 9") Suggested Retail: $16.95(sc)/$34.99(hc) ISBN: 978-1-7341546-5-8 (hc)

Throughout the 1960s and 1970s the Italian film industry cranked out over 600 "Spaghetti Westerns" and for every *Fistful of Dollars* were a dozen pale imitations, some of them hilarious. Many of these lesser known Spaghettis are available in bargain bin DVD packs and stream for free online. If ever you've wondered which are worth your time and which aren't, this is the book for you. Softcover (160pp./5.06" X 7.8") Suggested Retail: $9.99

123

THE LOST FILMS FANZINE PRESENTS MOVIE MILESTONES #3

THE BICEP BOOKS CATALOGUE

MOVIES UNMADE SERIES

Kong Unmade explores unproduced scripts like *King Kong vs. Frankenstein* (1958), unfinished films like *The Lost Island* (1934), and lost movies like *King Kong Appears in Edo* (1938). As a bonus, all the Kong rip-offs like *Konga* (1961) and *Queen Kong* (1976) are reviewed. Hardcover (350 pp/5.83" X 8.27")/Softcover (376 pp/5.5" X 8.5") Suggested Retail: $24.99(hc)/$19.99 (sc) ISBN: 978-1-7341546-2-7(hc)

Jaws Unmade explores unproduced scripts like *Jaws 3, People 0* (1979), abandoned ideas like a Quint prequel, and even aborted sequels to Jaws inspired movies like *Orca Part II*. As a bonus, all the Jaws rip-offs like *Grizzly* (1976) and *Tentacles* (1977) are reviewed. Hardcover (316 pp/5.83" X 8.27")/Softcover (340 pp/5.5" X 8.5") Suggested Retail: $29.99(hc)/$17.95 (sc) ISBN: 978-1-7344730-1-8(hc)

Coming in 2021, *Classic Monsters Unmade* will cover lost and unmade films starring Dracula, Frankenstein, the Mummy and more monsters from Universal, Hammer, and beyond. Covers everything from *The Wolf Man vs. Dracula* to *Frankenstein vs. Godzilla*. Alternate versions of completed movies like *Frankenstein Meets the Wolfman* and *Horror of Dracula* will also be covered.

NOSTALGIA

Written at an intermediate reading level for the kid in all of us, these picture books will take you back to your youth. In the spirit of the old Ian Thorne books are covered *Giant Apes of the Movies*, *Dinosauruses of the Movies* and *Monster Insects of the Movies*.

Hardcover/Softcover (44 pp/7.5" X 9.25") Suggested Retail: $17.95(hc)/ $9.99(sc) ISBN: 978-1-7341546-9-6 (hc) 978-1-7344730-5-6 (sc)

Hardcover/Softcover (44 pp/7.5" X 9.25") Suggested Retail: $17.95(hc)/ $9.99(sc) ISBN: 978-1-7344730-6-3 (hc) 978-1-7344730-7-0 (sc)

Hardcover/Softcover (44 pp/7.5" X 9.25") Suggested Retail: $17.95(hc)/ $9.99(sc) ISBN: 978-1-7347816-3-2 (hc) 978-1-7347816-2-5(sc)

THE BICEP BOOKS CATALOGUE

CRYPTOZOOLOGY/COWBOYS & SAURIANS

Cowboys & Saurians: Prehistoric Beasts as Seen by the Pioneers explores dinosaur sightings from the pioneer period via real newspaper reports from the time. Well-known cases like the Tombstone Thunderbird are covered along with more obscure cases like the Crosswicks Monster and more. Softcover (357 pp/5.06" X 7.8") Suggested Retail: $19.95 ISBN: 978-1-7341546-1-0

Cowboys & Saurians: Ice Age zeroes in on snowbound saurians like the Ceratosaurus of the Arctic Circle and a Tyrannosaurus of the Tundra, as well as sightings of Ice Age megafauna like mammoths, glyptodons, Sarkastodons and Saber-toothed tigers. Tales of a land that time forgot in the Arctic also covered. Softcover (264 pp/5.06" X 7.8") Suggested Retail: $14.99 ISBN: 978-1-7341546-7-2

Southerners & Saurians takes the series formula of exploring newspaper accounts of monsters in the pioneer period with an eye to the Old South. In addition to dinosaurs are covered Lizardmen, Frogmen, giant leeches and mosquitoes, and the Dingocroc, which might be an alien rather than a prehistoric survivor. Softcover (202 pp/5.06" X 7.8") Suggested Retail: $13.99 ISBN: 978-1-7344730-4-9

UFOLOGY/THE REAL COWBOYS & ALIENS IN CONJUNCTION WITH ROSWELL BOOKS

The Real Cowboys and Aliens: Early American UFOs explores UFO sightings in the USA between the years 1899-1864. Stories of encounters sometimes involved famous figures in U.S. history such as Lewis and Clark, and Thomas Jefferson. Hardcover (242pp/6" X 9") Softcover (262 pp/5.06" X 7.8") Suggested Retail: $24.99 (hc)/$15.95(sc) ISBN: 978-1-7341546-8-9 (hc)/978-1-7344730-8-7 (sc)

The second entry in the series, *Old West UFOs*, covers reports spanning the years 1865-1895. Includes tales of Men in Black, Reptilians, Spring-Heeled Jack, Sasquatch from space, and other alien beings, in addition to the UFOs and airships. Hardcover (276 pp/6" X 9") Softcover (308 pp/5.06" X 7.8") Suggested Retail: $29.95 (hc)/$17.95 (sc) ISBN: 978-1-7344730-0-1 (hc)/ 978-1-7344730-2-5 (sc)

The third entry in the series, *The Coming of the Airships*, encompasses a short time frame with an incredibly high concentration of airship sightings between 1896-1899. The famous Aurora, Texas, UFO crash of 1897 is covered in depth along with many others. Hardcover (196 pp/6" X 9") Softcover (222 pp/5.06" X 7.8") Suggested Retail: $24.99 (hc)/$15.95 (sc) ISBN: 978-1-7347816-1-8 (hc)/ 978-1-7347816-0-1(sc)

BACK ISSUES

THE LOST FILMS FANZINE

ISSUE #1 SPRING 2020 The lost Italian cut of *Legend of Dinosaurs and Monster Birds* called *Terremoto 10 Grado*, plus *Bride of Dr. Phibes* script, *Good Luck! Godzilla*, the King Kong remake that became a car commercial, Bollywood's lost *Jaws* rip-off, Top Ten Best Fan Made Godzilla trailers plus an interview with Scott David Lister. 60 pages. Three variant covers/editions (premium color/basic color/b&w)

ISSUE #2 SUMMER 2020 How 1935's *The Capture of Tarzan* became 1936's *Tarzan Escapes*, the Orca sequels that weren't, Baragon in Bollywood's *One Million B.C.*, unmade *Kolchak: The Night Stalker* movies, *The Norliss Tapes, Superman V: The New Movie*, why there were no *Curse of the Pink Panther* sequels, *Moonlight Mask: The Movie*. 64 pages. Two covers/editions (basic color/b&w)

ISSUE #3 FALL 2020 Blob sequels both forgotten and unproduced, *Horror of Dracula* uncut, *Frankenstein Meets the Wolfman* and talks, myths of the lost *King Kong* Spider-Pit sequence debunked, *Carnosaur* novel vs. the movies, *Terror in the Streets* 50th anniversary, *Bride of Godzilla* 55th Unniversary, Lee Powers sketchbook. 100 pages. Two covers/editions (basic color/b&w)

ISSUE #4 WINTER 2020/21 *Diamonds Are Forever's* first draft with Goldfinger, *Disciple of Dracula* into *Brides of Dracula*, *War of the Worlds That Weren't Part II*, *Day the Earth Stood Still II* by Ray Bradbury, *Deathwish 6, Atomic War Bride, What Am I Doing in the Middle of a Revolution?*, *Spring Dream in the Old Capital* and more. 70 pages. Two covers/editions (basic color/basic color/b&w)

MOVIE MILESTONES

ISSUE #1 AUGUST 2020 Debut issue celebrating 80 years of *One Million B.C.* (1940), and an early 55th Anniversary for *One Million Years B.C.* (1966). Abandoned ideas, casting changes, and deleted scenes are covered, plus, a mini-B.C. stock-footage filmography and much more! 54 pages. Three collectible covers/editions (premium color/basic color/b&w)

ISSUE #2 OCTOBER 2020 Celebrates the joint 50th Anniversaries of *When Dinosaurs Ruled the Earth* (1970) and *Creatures the World Forgot* (1971). Also includes looks at *Prehistoric Women* (1967), *When Women Had Tails* (1970), and *Caveman* (1981), plus unmade films like *When the World Cracked Open*. 72 pages. Three collectible covers/editions (premium color/basic color/b&w)

ISSUE #3 WINTER 2021 Japanese 'Panic Movies' like *The Last War* (1961), *Submersion of Japan* (1973), and *Bullet Train* (1975) are covered on celebrated author Sakyo Komatsu's 90th birthday. The famous banned Toho film *Prophecies of Nostradamus* (1974) are also covered. 124 pages. Three collectible covers/editions (premium color/basic color/ b&w)

ISSUE #4 SPRING 2021 This issue celebrates the joint 60th Anniversaries of *Gorgo, Reptilicus* and *Konga* examining unmade sequels like *Reptilicus 2*, and other related lost projects like *Kuru Island* and *The Volcano Monsters*. Also explores the Gorgo, Konga and Reptilicus comic books from Charlton. 72 pages. Three collectible covers/editions (premium color/basic color/b&w)

www.ingramcontent.com/pod-product-compliance
Lightning Source LLC
Chambersburg PA
CBHW031136120525
26538CB00039B/847